W9-AUO-684

JUDAISM

A Religion of Deeds and Ideals

JUDAISM
A Religion of
Deeds and Ideals

David C. Gross

HIPPOCRENE BOOKS
New York

For information, address:
HIPPOCRENE BOOKS, INC.
171 Madison Avenue
New York, NY 10016

ISBN 0-87052-068-7

Library of Congress Cataloging-in-Publication Data is available.

Printed in the United States of America.

For Esther

CONTENTS

PREFACE

JUDAISM HAS BEEN DESCRIBED AS THE MOTHER FAITH, AND Christianity and Islam as the daughter religions of Judaism.

And it was Mohammed himself who pinned the phrase "the people of the book" on the Jews.

Judaism has existed for nearly four thousand years, growing from a single man (Abraham) in search of the true God into a vast community. Its people fled slavery in Egypt, wandered for forty years through the wilderness, where Moses received the Torah. At last they settled in the Promised Land, remaining independently resolute and alone in their belief in monotheism for nearly fifteen hundred years, after which Christianity, and later Islam, also proclaimed their belief in one God.

Their centrally located country defeated by the powerful Romans, the adherents of Judaism—the Jews—were exiled to the four corners of the world, where they have lived for nearly two millenia. Only in the latter half of the twentieth century has there developed a serious effort to enable the Jews to return to their ancient homeland.

During the last two thousand years, in virtually every corner of Europe, Asia, and North Africa, Jews have been brutally persecuted, expelled, forcibly converted, massacred—because they refused to give up their faith.

The story of Judaism therefore is a story of heroism and martyrdom, of oppression and cruelty, and of courage and abiding faith.

What is Judaism that it has persisted for so long? What is its intrinsic message that so many have preferred death to conversion?

There is nothing dogmatic about Judaism. No one can say that it is the following of ten principles, and then add a period, and say that's it. Judaism is alive and dynamic; it is based on certain clear-cut precepts but it believes in adapting to changing conditions, in meeting the challenges of the day and fulfilling the needs of its adherents, the Jews.

Since Judaism has persisted for so long, and since the Jewish people—despite overwhelming assaults and persecutions—have managed to survive, what is their secret?

The answer, I believe, is many-faceted: Judaism is honest, realistic, pragmatic, adaptable, idealistic, challenging, and fulfilling—all at once. Perhaps most important: if a Jew practices Judaism fully and sincerely, committed to the prophetic principles of ethical conduct and observant of the ritual practices, he will discover in himself a sense of spiritual serenity that is so sadly lacking in our day.

I hope a hint of this inner peace which derives from Judaism will be conveyed to every reader.

D. C. G.

CHAPTER ONE
ANCIENT ORIGINS

JUDAISM IS THE RELIGION OF THE JEWISH PEOPLE. IT IS A faith that had its beginnings early, some four thousand years ago. Both Christianity and Islam, each with hundreds of millions of adherents throughout the world, acknowledge that they are in a very real sense offshoots of the mother faith, of Judaism.

To judge from the attention that the world's popular media, and literature itself, pay to the subject of Jews and therefore of Judaism, someone uninformed might believe that Judaism too has tens of millions, if not hundreds of millions, of followers.

The facts are phenomenally different:

—There are perhaps thirteen million Jews in the world, of whom nearly one-half reside in the United States. (Israel is second in terms of Jewish population, followed by the Soviet Union, France, and Britain.)

—A large number of Jews, perhaps one-half or even more, do not think of themselves as "religious." They consider themselves secular or cultural Jews. By and large these people have not renounced the Jewish religion; on the contrary, they usually admire its ethical and moral precepts and tend to claim

1

that they are firm believers in Judaism's moral teachings—but they reject ritual observance, attendance at synagogue services, the Jewish dietary laws, and other manifestations of a religious way of life.

—Oddly, even among those Jews who proclaim themselves to be "religious," there are quite a few who, in their heart of hearts, are skeptical of Judaism's hard-core beliefs. Such people will often be regular worshipers at Sabbath or holiday services. They will celebrate the various Jewish holidays, keep a kosher home, fast on Yom Kippur—and yet, if pressed for an answer as to whether they believe there is a God, will declare: "I don't know—I think so, I hope so."

* * *

An historian once described the Jewish people as a community that, for nearly four thousand years, has been in search of God.

Martin Buber, the world-famous theologian of the twentieth century, when once asked to define Judaism responded that he could not put it into words. Many have tried to explain what Judaism is:

—One thing is clear: one cannot attempt to define Judaism without recounting the history of the Jewish people. Each is inextricably interwoven with the other.

—Abraham Joshua Heschel, one of the great religious teachers of the twentieth century, stressed that Judaism is a "religion of time"; it seeks to hallow time. The Sabbaths, he taught, "are our great cathedrals."

—Abba Hillel Silver, an outstanding American rabbi and Zionist leader, said that Judaism rejects everything that is "extreme and excessive," or that "deifies man or degrades him."

—Samson Raphael Hirsch, a nineteenth-century religious spokesman, taught that Judaism's "most cherished ideal is the universal brotherhood of mankind."

—The French writer, Edmond Fleg, who at one stage in his

life almost decided to leave the Jewish community, wrote that Judaism is "faith in the progress of man" which will lead to the "kingdom of God."

* * *

In a unique tribute to the Jewish people, the scholar Paul Johnson (in his book, *A History of the Jews*) has written that the Jews are the "most tenacious people in history." Jews are ambivalent towards the possession of land, he writes. "No race has maintained over so long a period of time so emotional an attachment to a particular corner of the earth's surface" as have the Jews towards the Holy Land. And yet, he adds, "it is a curious fact that for more than three-quarters of their existence as a race, a majority of Jews have always lived outside the land they call their own. They do so today."

* * *

Historians, scholars, theologians, thoughtful people everywhere cannot help but wonder about Judaism and the Jewish people: how did this small people survive for four thousand years despite massacres, pogroms, forced conversions, expulsions, assimilation, homelessness, abject poverty?

There were outstanding ancient peoples who came from the same general region as the Jews, the Middle East, a region that is the crossroads of three continents. The Sumerians, Babylonians, Assyrians, Mesopotamians—they are all gone, swallowed up in the mists of history. But the Jewish people, and therefore Judaism, remain; if anything, in spite of the calamity of the Holocaust during which six million Jews—one-third of the total Jewish community—were destroyed, the Jewish people today is stronger, more vibrant, more creative, more certain of its place in world society.

Why? How is one to explain this phenomenon?

Traditional Jewish thinkers have no problem with this question. The Jews, they state without hesitation, were chosen by God to carry out a special task—to spread the message of universal brotherhood and peace to every corner of the world. When this message has been fully disseminated, a messianic era will ensue for all mankind, in which peace, compassion, justice, loving-kindness will prevail, and war, dissension, cruelty, and poverty will come to a permanent end.

Not all Jews will agree with this assessment. Noting that the Bible describes the Jews as a "stiff-necked" people, some will argue that the Jewish people has persisted and thrived because Jews are determined, stubborn, intelligent, and because history has taught them to survive in a world of terror and violence.

Martin Gilbert, the British historian, put it well when he sought to understand the Jews' unique ability to retain their identity through the centuries, despite the vast array of oppressive factors confronting them. He attributes the Jews' staying power to their adherence to their faith, and then goes on to explain what Judaism was, and still is:

"The Jews' unique religious system," he writes in the *Illustrated Atlas of Jewish Civilization,* "is more than a religion. Besides the belief in a single, indivisible deity, it embraces a set of ethical and moral precepts covering every aspect of daily life—from hygiene and behavior, to justice and equality before God and the law.

"Not all the concepts that make up what is known as Judaism were new and original—many were echoes of other ancient cultures—but it was the Jews who brought them together for the first time. Although the Jews have always been a minority in all lands outside Israel, the sheer power of these concepts has contributed to the shaping of both Christianity and Islam, as well as inspiring the secular philosophy of the west. Jerusalem itself is a center of three world religions."

* * *

According to the Bible and Jewish tradition, Judaism begins with Abraham, a man from Ur (in what is today southern Iraq) to whom God personally spoke, ordering him to go west to the land of Canaan, there to found a great people, and to teach that people the belief in one God. Some of the biblical stories that precede God's choosing of Abraham—the flood and Noah and the ark; the divine demand of the ultimate sacrifice, the binding of Isaac; and later the discovery of an infant in the reeds of a river, who turns out to be Moses—are all stories with parallels among the ancient Mesopotamians. The Jews, however, offered them not as myths, but enveloped them in a religious tradition, elevating them, through commentaries and interpretations, to higher spiritual plateaus.

Through the sagacious explanations of the rabbis, over the centuries these biblical stories took on religious meanings which bolstered the spirit of the Jews during times of distress and strengthened their commitment to an ethical lifestyle in more peaceful periods.

The principal founders of what eventually came to be known as Judaism are the patriarchs Abraham, Isaac, Jacob, and of course Moses, the great lawgiver. Each of these giants of the Bible, separately and in his own way, discovered God and came to be an avid believer in, and exponent of, monotheism, Judaism's most important primary teaching.

Abraham is thus considered to be the first Jew; his son Isaac and his grandson Jacob followed in his religious footsteps. The early Hebrews were a nomadic people, always seeking better grazing and farming land. Jacob (whose name was changed to Israel after he fought through the night with a superhuman being or angel) was the progenitor of the main body of the Jewish people—the twelve tribes of Israel were descended from his ten sons and two grandsons (the sons of Joseph).

The biblical narrative of this period is generally well-known: how Joseph was sold into slavery by his brothers; how he came to interpret the dreams of the pharoah and correctly forecast that seven years of agricultural bounty would be followed by seven lean years; how he was named to the second highest post in Egypt; how his family joined him in Egypt because famine had ravaged their own homeland; how the Hebrews, at first honored and respected, were later enslaved and grew to a multitude of six hundred thousand; and how Moses led this vast populace out of Egypt, across the wilderness (presumably Sinai) and, after forty years, they reached the Promised Land, the territory from which they had been exiled for several hundred years.

It was while the Israelites were in the wilderness that the elevation of the Jewish people to a religious community first began. It was at Mount Sinai, during this time, that the ancient Jews first received the *Torah,* generally translated as the Hebrew Bible.

This seminal moment in Jewish history is known as the Revelation. Moses was commanded by God to ascend Mount Sinai, and there God gave him the Torah. To this day the Giving of the Law at Mount Sinai is celebrated annually during the *Shavuot* (Pentecost) holiday, which generally falls in late May or June.

Orthodox Jews believe that Moses received the entire Torah at Sinai; others interpret the revelation as a historic moment when God gave Moses the Ten Commandments. Still others believe that Moses ascended Sinai and there, under divine inspiration, composed either the Decalogue, or the Torah, in whole or in part.

There are even some commentators who believe that every Jew, those already born and those yet to be born, stood at the foot of Mount Sinai and joined in receiving the Torah.

However one interprets that momentous event, the fact is that the Revelation marked the opening of a new chapter in Jewish history—when the Jewish people was transformed from a community that believed in one God into a full-fledged religious community that saw its very existence as founded on a three-part base: belief in God, commitment to the laws and precepts of the Torah, and a strong sense of Jewish nationhood.

One could say that the Jews who came to Egypt in search of

sustenance were a small, pastoral group with a then unique belief in one God; when they left the Sinai wilderness en route to the Promised Land, they were a large nation endowed with a prophetic, universalistic religious faith that taught mercy, justice, kindness, peace and a life of the spirit and of the heart.

* * *

Certainly there are many concepts in Judaism that are similar to those of other religions. Moreover, since Judaism is a faith or way of life without a clerical hierarchy—rabbis are essentially teachers; they can instruct and interpret, but they cannot issue edicts or rulings unless based on Jewish religious law—there are often competing, and even conflicting interpretations of Jewish law. Ultimately, however, it is biblical law or talmudic law that determines how a particular issue is to be decided.

The word *Torah* in its narrowest sense refers to the first third of the Jewish Bible. It is sometimes translated as the Pentateuch, or the Five Books of Moses, and consists of the following volumes: Genesis, Exodus, Leviticus, Numbers, and Deuteronomy. The other two-thirds of the Jewish Bible are the *Prophets* (Isaiah, Jeremiah, Ezekiel, Joshua, Judges, Samuel I and II, Kings I and II) and the *Writings,* sometimes referred to as the Holy Writings, or *Ketuvim* in Hebrew (composed of Psalms, Proverbs, Job, Song of Songs, Ruth, Lamentations, Ecclesiastes, Esther, Daniel, Ezra, Nehemiah and Chronicles I and II). Included in the prophetic section are short contributions from twelve minor figures: Hosea, Joel, Amos, Obadiah, Jonah, Micah, Nahum, Habakuk, Zephaniah, Hagai, Zechariah, and Malachi.

In its broadest sense, the word *Torah* is all-encompassing: it can mean all of Judaism, or all the teachings of the Bible together with the talmudic and midrashic commentaries that have come down through the centuries. Thus, when a devout young man announces that he plans to commit his life to the study of Torah, he may very well mean that he hopes to absorb into his mind and soul all the teachings, interpretations and comments of vast numbers of sages and rabbis over a period of at least two millenia who themselves have spent lifetimes seeking to master the wisdom, insights, precepts of Judaism.

As anyone who is familiar with the Jewish Bible knows, it is a quite marvelous document that calls out for study, preferably with a gifted teacher, rather than for intense reading or easy perusal. It is not unusual for a class of students, teenagers or adults, to sit together on a summer afternoon and, through reading, discussion and even debate, probe to determine the precise meaning of a sentence or two comprising a tiny part of a single biblical verse.

The Torah however is only the second of the three-part basis that underpins Judaism. First and foremost is the belief in God.

A fundamental principle of Judaism is absolute faith in the existence of God, a belief that there is and always will be a Supreme Being, and that, although people have freedom of choice and can opt either to lead lives of great kindness or to conduct themselves in a cruel, barbaric and ruthless manner, in the end they will be judged and either rewarded or punished by God.

Judaism is aware of the fact that there are religious groups that do not believe in a divine being, and that there are people, who are the epitome of kindness and compassion, who profess not to believe in any divinity. There is even a small group of Jews who refer to themselves as humanists and totally reject all the religious trappings of Judaism, focusing solely on Judaism's ethical teachings.

The pendulum of belief in a Supreme Being has historically swung back and forth, sometimes with surprising results. When Albert Einstein was asked if he believed in God, he replied that he was convinced that there is a Supreme Intelligence, and that the world as we know it did not come about just by happenstance. Then there are the cases of Jews who survived the Nazi death camps. Some came out cursing God and rejecting completely all religious talk or observance; and some came out newly-religious, anxious to begin life afresh as observant Jews who follow every law, every ruling, every concept of Judaism. There were rabbis who survived and lost their faith entirely, and there were some rabbis who emerged from the death camps with new religious vigor.

In Judaism, a religion that stresses deeds rather than creeds, being a religious Jew has numerous aspects. First, it is a declaration of commitment to the Jewish community, of expressing concern for its welfare and well-being. Second, it is a way of life that emphasizes continued learning, and for many Jews this is the essence of Judaism. They will study Torah daily if possible, listen to their rabbi's sermon, which is often a commentary on the week's biblical reading. They will enroll in adult classes at the synagogue or the Jewish community center, anxious to expand their knowledge and comprehension. If this pursuit of learning also involves a certain amount of formal public prayer in the synagogue, some of these people contend, then so be it. It is not a high price to pay for the privilege of remaining culturally, intellectually young. There are also some Jews who are not assiduous in the pursuit of study, and neither are they particularly anxious to attend religious services, but what draws them to the synagogue, and to the religious community, are the social encounters. To put it another way: many people do not especially enjoy their working hours; they crave social banter with people of their choice, and since few Jews frequent bars, they gravitate instead towards meetings and other functions arranged by the men's clubs (the women move toward the synagogue's sisterhood), largely for the friendships that evolve, for the social contact with their peers.

Thus, belief in God is often held by people whose faith is actually attenuated, but who apparently enjoy certain other aspects of being Jews.

The second basic foundation of Judaism, Torah, is more difficult for many people to articulate. At a synagogue service on the Sabbath or on a holiday, when the Torah (the Pentateuch, written by hand on special sheets of calf skin) is paraded through the synagogue, most people will kiss the scroll and show their reverence for it. The truth, however, is that the overwhelming majority of Jews nowadays only pay lip service to study of the Torah. In the view of these people, Torah study is best left to the rabbis and advanced yeshiva students—a view that is diametrically opposed to the Jewish tradition which holds that every person, the learned and the not-so-learned, must devote time to studying the Torah.

Most Jews today believe that there definitely is a connection between God and the Jewish people, which was hallowed for all time when the Torah was handed to them at Sinai. Nonetheless, there is an overwhelming majority of Jews who shy away from regular study themselves. Among the orthodox, of course, there is a much larger percentage of people who do opt to study Torah regularly, over many years.

It is the third part of the basis for Judaism with which Jews generally find themselves most at ease: the concept of the special role of the Jewish people in world affairs. Jews may possess only a weak belief in a divine being, and they may seldom pray or follow Jewish rituals, but they almost invariably take pride in their concern for the welfare of the Jewish people.

Some people will explain that because Jews are so small in number, they look upon fellow Jews almost as distant relatives. Indeed, there is an ingrained Jewish tradition: *Kol Yisrael araivin zeh bazeh*—all Jews feel responsible for one another. To this must be added the almost mystical belief held by many Jews, namely, that God did choose the Jews to spread His message and therefore every Jew must be regarded as a precious, divine emissary.

CHAPTER TWO
BELIEF IN GOD

BELIEF IN GOD IS ONE OF THE FOUNDATIONS OF JUDAISM. This faith in God, however, must be genuine, not merely arrived at through religious instruction, family tradition or a rejection of atheism. It should be instead a faith that is built on thoughtfulness, study and conviction.

A person who looks at the world around him cannot help but reach the conclusion that somehow a Supreme Being conceived and created everything we see—the daily sunrise and sundown, the trees and shrubs and flowers, the clouds and the oceans, the seasonal weather changes, the lowly ants and insects, and the mighty lions and elephants.

The human being is an absolute miracle of creation. Each person has a heart, a brain, arms, legs; we grow from infancy into adulthood, and our minds expand as our limbs and muscles grow. People can be taught to read, to calculate, to sing and dance, to entertain, to teach, to cure the sick, to paint and sculpt, to plant a tree, to write words that enthrall and inform—the believer in God asks the non-believer: is all of life around us an accident? Did not a Supreme Being plan it all, and does He not direct the world?

The response of the non-believer, to Judaism and to other faiths, is often linked to the evil that continues to exist in the world. If there really is a God, the atheist retorts, then why is there so much cruelty, why is there dread disease, why are good people struck down in the prime of life while evil individuals apparently continue to thrive?

For Jews, especially in the twentieth century, this question of evil and the absence of God is acute. Many Jews ask about the Holocaust that took place in central Europe between 1933 and 1945—where was God? Why did God permit the massacre of one and a half million Jewish children and four and a half million Jewish adults? What was their sin?

These are not easy questions to answer; some Jews declare that God turned His face away during the Holocaust. Others maintain that we humans are simply not capable of comprehending God's plan. There are even some extremists who insist that the Holocaust took place because God was displeased that Jews, by and large, were not observing all the religious laws and regulations.

Confronted by the dilemma of where God was during the Holocaust years, most Jews maintain that they have no answer; and then hasten to add that they prefer not to have an explicit response and continue to live as committed Jews rather than adopt a totally atheistic lifestyle. A life without belief in God, these people say, is empty, it is devoid of meaning—in other words, it would imply that we are born, we live, we die, and that's the end of it. That is not acceptable, there has to be a more meaningful dimension of life, a deeper purpose, and although we may not be able to grasp it now, in the course of time this higher meaning will hopefully become clearer.

Another way to look at the problem of Judaism and God is to bear in mind that the Bible teaches Jews that they are to become a "holy people," a "kingdom of priests." Jews may very well feel that even though they themselves do not understand why evil exists in the world, there has to be some kind of acceptable reason—for after all, Jews must continue to strive to become holy, and how can one become holy unless there is genuine faith in God?

Belief in God is a problem that has confronted thoughtful people through the centuries. To fully understand the background of this issue, we should first turn to the early biblical passages where Abraham proclaims the existence of one God. For his time and place, this was a startling, revolutionary idea; Abraham knew that all around him people worshiped a multiplicity of gods—idols that were supposed to assure a good harvest, or protect against devastating storms, or ensure the well-being of a man's family. Abraham's new concept of one God, who was invisible, was a dramatic departure from these traditions. That is why Judaism has what amounts to a declaration of faith, a brief statement that is recited twice daily at religious services—and the same statement is pronounced by a person who feels his life ebbing away.

This statement, known as the *Shma*, declares simply: "Hear O Israel, the Lord our God, the Lord is one." The word *one* is an oblique slap at the continuing pagan worship of many gods. The word *one* in this context also has a deeper significance—it can be explained as *unique*, i.e., that there are no comparable deities, God is the supreme ruler and master, and no other being or idea can be likened to Him.

Furthermore, in Judaism, God is not only one and unique but He is also eternal. He has always been in the universe and He will always be there. If we do not always understand His actions, this is solely because we are mortal beings while He is divine and thus beyond our understanding.

The great Jewish physician-philosopher Maimonides, who lived and wrote his immortal works a thousand years ago, is considered to be the most rational and logical of Jewish religious commentators. When he was confronted with the age-old problem of a man's freedom of choice, he was forced to admit that he could not find an acceptable solution. The issue is simple to formulate: if God knows everything about everyone (i.e., He possesses foreknowledge of man's actions), then how can it be said that a person really has freedom of choice—to choose the righteous way of life and not to follow his evil inclinations. After wrestling with the problem for a long time, Maimonides said that a good Jew (i.e., one who follows the teachings and the rules of Judaism), must continue to believe both that God has foreknowledge of what people will do during their lifetime, and that each person nonetheless possesses freedom of choice and can choose a righteous path.

Perhaps that is why one of Judaism's principal tenets addresses the question of repentance. In the Jewish view, a person—no matter how sinful—can always repent and start anew. The prophets of old—Jeremiah, Isaiah and Ezekiel—were always castigating the people of their time to repent. "Make you a new heart and a new spirit, for why will you die, O House of Israel?" Ezekiel said. And the Baal Shem Tov, the founder of the Hassidic movement, who lived in the eighteenth century, taught that "each penitent's thought is like the voice of God."

* * *

Can a Jew be considered—by himself or by others—as a good Jew, and still have doubts about God?

Rabbi Emanuel Rackman, one of America's outstanding rabbinical figures and now the chancellor of Bar-Ilan University in Israel, puts it this way: "God may have His own reasons for denying us certainty with regard to His existence and nature. One reason apparent to us is that man's certainty with regard to anything is poison to his soul. Who knows this better than modern man, who has had to cope with dogmatic fascists, communists, and even scientists?"

The late Milton Steinberg, a memorable American rabbi who influenced numerous students of the rabbinate prior to his untimely passing, said that "if the believer has his troubles with evil, the atheist has more and graver difficulties to contend with. Reality stumps him altogether, leaving him baffled

14

not by one consideration but by many, from the existence of natural law through the instinctual cunning of the insect to the brain of the genius and the heart of the prophet. This then is the intellectual reason for believing in God: That, though this belief is not free from difficulties, it stands out, head and shoulders, as the best answer to the riddle of the universe."

If a visitor were to enter a synagogue on *Yom Kippur*, the Day of Atonement, the holiest day of the year in the Jewish calendar, he would find a congregation of men, women and children clad in their best holiday clothes, worshiping and praying together from the special holiday prayerbook and feeling a little uplifted, at least for that particular day until the fast ends with the sounding of the *shofar* (ram's horn).

Suppose that the visitor were able to take a poll of the congregants, and ask whether they believed in God, and if they saw in God a personal God; or whether they were there for non-religious purposes, i.e., because they felt that, as members of the Jewish community, they should participate in Yom Kippur services and join in the traditional fast, and in that manner express their solidarity with the Jewish people. Chances are that to the question, do you believe in a personal God?, there would be a wide variety of replies. Perhaps as many as 50 percent would respond with a definite yes; another 20–30 percent might fudge and avoid the answer; and the remainder would reluctantly say no.

For, although a total, unequivocal belief in God as the Supreme Being, as the omnipotent ruler of the universe, certainly exists among Jews, there is also a sizable number of Jews who are skeptical of the concept, but who nevertheless choose to remain actively Jewish because of two particular attitudes that have been deeply absorbed. Firstly, that the Jewish people must be a holy people, and this sense of holiness and specialness permeates most Jews' innermost feelings about Judaism; secondly, that Judaism is deed-, not creed-oriented. There is a strong tradition that mankind is co-creator with God, and that there is an abiding need to ameliorate suffering,

improve society, and in general make this a better world. It is
this deed-oriented philosophy that accounts for the fact that
Jews are often exceptionally active in movements designed to
better society, and that explains the disproportionately high
degree of philanthropy that is to be found in the Jewish
community. The ancient Hebrew maxim expresses this viewpoint sharply: *Lo ha'medrash, elah ha'ma'aseh*—not words, but
actions, count.

Understanding the very existence of God is seen by Maimonides as limited by mankind's limitations. He wrote: "We
understand only that He exists, not His essence." He also said
that the "foundation and pillar of all wisdom is to recognize
that there is an original Being, and that all exist only through
the reality of His being."

Some thirty centuries ago the saintly Rabbi Akiba said that
"as a house implies a builder, a dress a weaver, a door a
carpenter, so the world proclaims God, its Creator."

There are some people who are willing to accept the idea of
the existence of God, but have trouble explaining the meaning
of God. Thus, for example, Leo Baeck, a leading German
rabbi who survived the Nazi concentration camp There-
sienstadt, said that "it is in God that morality has its foundation and guarantee." To him, the concept of God was meant to
bolster the spread of moral teachings. A very different approach was taken by the popular writer Ben Hecht. He said
that a person who "writes of himself without speaking of God
is like someone who identifies himself without giving his
address."

Judaism and Jewish thinkers through the ages have recognized that the existence of God can be a serious challenge.
Many people explain that they wish to believe, indeed that
they would love to have a firm faith in God's existence, but
they find it very difficult, if not impossible. In his memoirs, the
poet Heinrich Heine said: "The most vital question of humanity is the existence of God." And Abraham Joshua Heschel

went even further: "God is of no importance unless He is of supreme importance."

In his *Thirteen Principles of Faith* Maimonides wrote that "I believe with perfect faith that the Creator . . . is not a body, is free from all properties of matter, and has no form whatever." In his classical *History,* Tacitus wrote, more than two millenia ago: "Jews worship with the mind alone. They believe in one God, supreme and immortal, and deem it impious . . . to fashion effigies of God after the likeness of man."

Judaism thus confirms that God exists, that He is eternal, non-corporeal, omnipresent, omnipotent, omniscient, just, merciful, benevolent, a healer, protective, a redeemer, the king of all, the father of us all. The Bible also teaches that man was created in the image of God, implying therefore that human beings should strive to emulate those qualities of goodness, justice, mercy, benevolence, that are attributed to God.

Judaism does not accept fatalism as a valid philosophy. As the Yiddish saying has it, the way we make up our bed, that's the way we'll sleep. On the other hand, Jews place enormous faith in the providential powers of God. In the biblical book of Proverbs we are told that "a man's heart devises his way, but the Lord directs his steps." Judaism expects its adherents to place their faith in God, as expressed in the immortal words of the Twenty-third Psalm: "The Lord is my shepherd, I shall not want." Many centuries later a Yiddish-speaking wit said that "man proposes, and God laughs."

In Jewish tradition, the closeness of God to mankind is felt very deeply. It is almost a physical sense of proximity. During religious services, especially in a traditional synagogue, it is not unusual to see men reciting the first part of the hallowed *Shma* prayer, their eyes shut tight, one hand covering their eyes, obviously lost in exaltation. When pressed as to whether they hoped "to see God" they are likely to smile, shake their heads, and say, "No, but I wanted for a moment at least to feel close to Him."

A talmudic sage, Joshua ben Levi, said, "let a man enter a synagogue and pray silently, and the Holy One listens, like a friend in whose ear one whispers a secret." The eighteenth-century commentator Moshe Luzzatto stated that "man came into the world in order to achieve nearness to God." In a recent edition of a Reform prayerbook there is a line that sums up man's closeness to God: "O Lord, Thou art as close to us as breathing and yet farther than the farthermost star."

Judaism encourages its adherents to develop a sense of closeness to God. The Bible teaches that man should obey the following rule: "I have set the Lord always before me." Thus, when a Jew recites the blessing over bread or wine or any other time, he customarily begins with the words, *Baruch atah Adonai*—Blessed Art Thou O Lord—as though he were thanking a close friend for his bounty. One of the great Hassidic rabbis, known as the Kotzker rebbe, taught: "Let God not be a stranger to you." The Talmud teaches: "Let your God be your companion."

Nevertheless, while Judaism advocates that Jews should feel close to God and should emulate His divine attributes here on earth, there is also a tradition of not blindly obeying all of God's commandments, if we feel that some wrong is being committed against mankind. There is a famous story of a rabbi in the old country who, every Yom Kippur, would absent himself from his congregation. It took time, but eventually the puzzle was solved: out in the forest there was an impoverished older widow who needed wood for her stove and other supplies, and the rabbi felt that it was more important to provide for her—and thus right a grievous wrong—than remain in the synagogue all day with his congregants. There is also a story of another old world congregation who found themselves one day in mourning for the victims of a pogrom. The worshipers assembled to pray for help and to seek divine guidance in their time of travail. Their rabbi had a different idea: instead of conducting a regular service he announced that the congregation were now to be considered judges, and that together they would all take God to a *din Torah*—a religious tribunal—and, in effect, put Him on trial for the terrible fate that had befallen the Jews.

Judaism can thus be summed up as a belief in ethical monotheism—the belief in one God, and the commitment to live an ethical life. All of the religious rules and regulations, the customs and ceremonies, the holidays and festivals, lifetime study of the sacred Jewish texts—everything is seen as leading to an ethical life, led in harmony with God and linked across the centuries with the Jewish people of the past and of the future.

In Jewish tradition monotheism alone, without the ethical factor, is unacceptable. Judaism believes that mankind should be elevated spiritually to a higher plane, closer to the angels, as it were, who are themselves, of course, closer to God. The famous story of Rabbi Hillel and the pagan bears retelling.

The pagan asked the saintly rabbi to tell him what the Torah was all about while he, the pagan, stood on one foot. Hillel replied at once: "Do not do unto others what you would not want them to do to you. All the rest is commentary—and now, go and study."

The biblical prophets, each in their own time, all demanded of the Jews the same things: righteousness, justice, compassion, holiness. These, the prophets insisted, are what God wants of people.

Are there highly ethical people who have no belief whatever in God? Of course. Are there "religious" people who disdain ethical behavior? Unfortunately, yes.

Thus, ethical monotheism is the goal, the desired aim, the standard we wish to attain if our lives are to be better, and if society as a whole is to benefit. Judaism insists that both elements—ethics and the belief in one God—are interwoven with one another and merit full support and adherence.

For many twentieth-century people, faith in God is difficult to achieve because they have been brought up on philosophies of rationalism. That is why so many rabbis nowadays urge their younger congregants to "make the leap of faith." There is a hard-core tradition in Judaism that when even people who are not religious begin to live as though they were, observing all the rules, seeking out higher ethical forms of behavior, then something positive will happen; the religious way of life will become second nature to these individuals, and perhaps through osmosis, or through some mystical process, faith will follow.

After World War II, there was found in a cellar in Cologne an inscription written by a Jew who had been hidden by a German family from certain death by the Nazis. The message he left says: "I believe in the sun even when it is not shining. I believe in love even when not feeling it. I believe in God even when He is silent."

The famed Hassidic master Rabbi Nachman of Bratislav taught that "where reason ends, faith begins."

Time and again newly-religious Jews have repeated the same phenomenon: they approached Judaism and Jewish living without a firm belief in God, and after living as committed Jews, studying the Torah, observing the commandments, they suddenly found that faith and belief in God had come. It was as though there were a giant jigsaw puzzle, and little by little all the pieces began to fit in. And the final piece was a certain, firm belief in God.

CHAPTER THREE
LIVING BY THE TORAH

THERE ARE CERTAIN ORTHODOX JEWS WHO PROCLAIM THAT their aim is to live as "Torah-true" Jews. To them, the word *Torah* means the vastness of Jewish teaching, which—when properly and fully absorbed—shows us how God wants us to lead our lives.

It is interesting to note that the word *Torah* stems from a Hebrew root meaning to shoot, or more precisely, to aim at a target. Thus, Torah becomes synonymous with straight shooting, with a goal in life. On the other hand, the Hebrew word for sin is related to the word that means to miss—thus, sinfulness can be seen as missing the mark.

Nowadays, when Jews speak of the Torah as a way of life they generally mean the two parts of that term—the written Torah, i.e., the Five Books of Moses found in the Bible; together with the oral Torah, which consists of the talmudic and rabbinic commentaries that expound and interpret biblical law.

Thus, one of the Ten Commandments declares that we are

21

to abstain from doing any work on the Sabbath. The question arises: what is meant by work? Is milking a cow on the Sabbath work? Is taking a leisurely drive in the country, work? The answers, and many more, are found in the talmudic and rabbinical commentaries and explications.

In a very real sense, the oral Torah is still being composed, even now. New problems arise almost daily in the realm of medical ethics, for example, or in radically new methods of reproduction. Many of these issues require study before decisions can be reached on how they are to be interpreted from a Torah viewpoint. Thus certain rabbis study new problems, new challenges, and sit and discuss these questions together, and eventually issue an opinion. This decision, or opinion, becomes yet another addition to the oral Torah, in the form of what is generally referred to as *Responsa*—responses to religious questions that require rabbinical study and decision.

In the final years of the twentieth century, many of these questions deal with such matters as kosher foods, artificial insemination, abortion, intermarriage. (For example: if a chemical food additive supplements a processed food, is that food still kosher, since the additive changes its makeup during the cooking process? Another example: a Gentile girl converts to Judaism and lives a thoroughly Jewish life with her husband and children. When her still-Gentile parent dies, does she have to recite the kaddish memorial prayer?)

*   *   *

The Torah scroll that is read out during services in the synagogue is surely one of the most sacred components of Judaism. A trained scribe (called a *sofer*), using special black ink and working on parchment sheets made from the hides of animals that are considered kosher for eating purposes, copies the entire Torah, i.e., the Five Books of Moses, in the Hebrew script—a task that will often take as much as a year. Each letter is perfectly clear and precise. No punctuation whatsoever is used, although guidelines are permitted, to enable the scribe to produce neat, even columns of script. The parchment sheets are then sewn together, and the continuous text is rolled into a scroll.

The Torah is read aloud in synagogue at Sabbath morning and holiday services; each Sabbath's weekly reading is called a *sedra,* or a *parsha.* On Monday and Thursday mornings and on Saturday afternoons, at synagogue services, small excerpts from the upcoming sedra are also read.

The Torah service provides for a number of people to share in the honor of reading the sedra. *P'teecha,* which means the opening, enables one, or sometimes two, people to open the Holy Ark in which the Torah scrolls are kept when not in use.

A *Baal-koreh* means the Torah reader, who must be someone skilled and knowledgeable since the scroll's text consists of consonants only—not only is there no punctuation, but all vowels are omitted too, a common practice in advanced Hebrew. *Gabai* is the word used for an usher in a synagogue; in the Torah reading service the gabai's chief role is to call up those people being honored with participation and accord them a blessing, and to ascertain (from a printed book complete with vowels and punctuation) that the Torah reader makes no mistake in his rendition. On Sabbath morning, a total of seven people are called to be honored during the reading; this number can be enlarged to accommodate additional honorees. The final, or eighth, honor is called *maftir,* which is usually reserved for a bar or bat mitzvah; in addition to the Torah reading, a suitable section from the prophetic books is read aloud by the maftir honoree.

When the reading is completed two people are called up to help put the Torah back in the ark: *hagba* and *g'lila,* the former meaning literally, he who raises, for it is traditional for the hagba to lift the Torah high in the air while the congregants sing, "this is the Torah that Moses gave to the children of Israel." After the hagba is seated, the g'lila—literally the roller—rolls the scroll tightly together, binds it, and then encloses it in a colorful, decorated mantle. The Torah is then returned to the ark, with the help of one or two people who have been honored with the p'teecha.

In most synagogues, the Torah is carried around the synagogue both before and after the reading. Often the rabbi and cantor will go along and greet the congregants, most of whom extend a kiss to the Torah, either via their fingers or (in the case of the men) via the fringes of their prayer shawls. (In Sephardic synagogues, congregants usually throw a kiss toward the Torah).

Generally, when the Torah is resting on a table and is being read aloud, congregants remain in their seats and follow the reading in printed Bibles. When the Torah is raised or carried, the worshipers will stand also, as a sign of respect and reverence.

Most synagogues possess a few scrolls. From time to time, a Torah scroll must be sent out for repairs; the reader will notice that some letters have begun to fade or flake off the parchment. Such a Torah is not considered kosher; it must be checked and corrected by a scribe, a task that could take many weeks, or even months.

Whenever a synagogue acquires a Torah scroll, it is a time for celebration. Often the congregation will escort the Torah outside the synagogue, form a circle under the sky around whoever is holding the scroll, and sing and dance. Some Torah scrolls are brand new and have been commissioned by a family that wishes to contribute to a particular synagogue; this is no small gift, for a Torah scroll can cost many thousands of dollars.

In recent years, certain Torah scrolls have been moved about in rather dramatic ways. For example, in New York City there was a time when the majority of the Jewish community lived in three boroughs, Manhattan, Brooklyn, and the Bronx. In recent years Jews, like many other people, have moved to the suburbs. This meant that they have had to sell synagogue buildings and take along the Torah scrolls to be used in new, suburban houses of worship.

Another unusual situation resulted from the second world war. The Nazis destroyed every synagogue they could, but in most cases they collected the Torah scrolls and sent them to a central depot in Prague; a "museum of Jewish decadence" was planned to be erected there, featuring the nearly two thousand Torah scrolls that had been assembled.

When the Nazis were defeated, the Torah scrolls were transferred to the basement of a large synagogue in London. There, slowly and painstakingly, scribes examined them to ensure that they were fit for use. And since the end of the war in 1945, hundreds of these reclaimed and repaired Torah scrolls have been dispatched to new synagogues in Israel, the United States, France and many other places, where they are now in regular use.

* * *

No matter where a worshiper attends services on the Sabbath or on a holiday, the reading of the Torah portion of the week is a high point. An almost mystical ambience develops when the reader begins his familiar chanting; worshipers know that this is the same Torah that their ancestors have been reading from, studying, and living by for thousands of years. One feels that the Torah reading carries on a powerful tradition, a link to the far past, a link to Jews everywhere who at that moment are also reading from the Torah, a sense of awe and majesty and peacefulness. If the Sabbath is an oasis in time, as has been said, then the Torah is a cooling, refreshing spring.

The weekly Torah readings are so organized that they last for one full year, from one *Simchat Torah* festival to another. On this joyous occasion (which usually falls in late September or early October), all the Torah scrolls are removed from the ark, and everyone is encouraged to carry a scroll around the synagogue, singing and dancing and being cheered on by onlookers.

The explosive exuberance of the holiday which is dedicated

to the Torah, gives Jews an opportunity to proclaim to the world: "This is our Jewish legacy to the world. We brought forth the Torah, it is a tree of life, it teaches us how to live with compassion to all, to do justly, to provide for the poor and those in need. Other peoples have made important contributions to society. This Torah, this blueprint for a good life, this is the Jewish people's contribution."

* * *

The word *Torah* is sometimes translated as "the law." This is not correct. The late British chief rabbi, Joseph Hertz, said that the "real Torah is not merely the written text of the Five Books of Moses; the real Torah is the meaning enshrined in that text, as expounded and unfolded by successive generations of sages and teachers in Israel."

The great Hassidic master, the Baal Shem Tov, taught that "the object of the whole Torah is that man should become a Torah himself." A millenium ago, Maimonides said: "All the commandments and exhortations in the Torah aim at conquering the desires of the body . . . The general object is the well-being of the soul and of the body."

A talmudic dictum advises Jews about the Torah: "Turn it again and again, for everything is in it; contemplate it, grow gray and old over it, and swerve not from it, for there is no greater good." The great German Jewish philosopher, Franz Rosenzweig, wrote that "when a Jew is attacked, he should not keep the Torah in front of him as a shield, but he is to keep himself as a shield in front of the Torah."

And yet, despite all the reverence and love that Jews have for the Torah, despite the fact that Jewish tradition holds that the Torah is God's manual to the Jewish people, Jews are cautioned not to worship the Torah, but to worship only God. We should have love for the Torah, Jews are told, but we must have both love of and fear of God. Fear, the rabbis explain, denotes awe and leads to worship; the Torah is God's instrument, and it is to be honored but not worshiped. That is why rabbis and scholars through the centuries have felt no compunction about interpreting and reinterpreting biblical passages sometimes offering radically different commentaries. In other words, the Torah is to be regarded as a living document whose laws are to be obeyed but they may be amended, explained anew, added to, and redefined.

Is it possible that the framers of the American Constitution understood this when they provided ways and means that would enable succeeding generations to reinterpret and redefine the laws of this land?

* * *

Most rabbis, especially those living in the fast-paced western world, know how difficult it is for busy people to take time to study the Torah. In response, they have developed various schemes whereby Jews can try to find a few hours in the week for Torah study. In the Wall Street area of New York City, for example, a weekly class is held by busy brokers and investors—they simply bring a sandwich, gather in someone's board room, and with a teacher (usually a rabbi), for an hour or two, surrounded by the skyscrapers of the financial capital of the world, consider the ethical problems revealed by a biblical verse, and debate moral, correct conduct.

Similar groups have begun to proliferate around the country, but these are the exception. Many Jews do not even attend synagogue services, except on the two days of Rosh Hashanah and on Yom Kippur. Yet there are substantial numbers who do attend Sabbath services regularly. They may not fully understand the thrust of the prayers, they may not really understand the cantorial chanting, and they may even after a while become inured to the repetitive bar and bat mitzvah celebrations that eat up time in every synagogue. But if these congregants are lucky, the rabbi will relate the weekly Torah reading to events of the day, or to issues that trouble his listeners, and thus succeed in making the Torah reading an exciting intellectual and spiritual journey. In this way Torah study will become an ingrained feature of people's lifestyle.

Since the entire Torah, the Five Books of Moses, is read aloud in the synagogue during the course of a year, it stands to reason that a typical worshiper may read the Torah forty, fifty times or more during his lifetime. People may wonder: doesn't it become tiresome, the same material, year in and year out?

That's the magic of Torah study. Somehow, at every different stage of life people find new insights in its ancient passages. Assuming, for example, that a youth of thirteen begins to attend synagogue services regularly, he will probably, at that age, pay closer attention to the narratives in the Bible than to anything else. Then, as he gets older, and life treats him well or badly, he matures, his understanding expands, and some of the lines he first read years ago now take on new meanings. Amazingly, this pattern continues throughout life, so that even when one enters the sixth decade, believing one knows all there is to know, suddenly a verse of the Torah will catch one up short, and one realizes how much more wisdom there is to master.

Rabbis emphasize that the study of the Torah is even more important than practicing its precepts—because study will lead to practice, and obeying biblical rules after mastering them indicates a thorough understanding of what is right and good. Oddly, there are some rabbis today who feel that the study of physics and philosophy are vital for young Jewish men and women, for these disciplines will lead to a greater appreciation of Torah study. Maimonides held the same viewpoint a thousand years ago; he was criticized then by certain rabbis just as some modern rabbis are berated for taking this broad view of Torah study. Back in talmudic days, some two millenia ago, there were great rabbis, such as Rabban Gamaliel, who believed that Torah study really means all of human learning. To prove his point, the rabbi hung on the wall of his study early sketches of what the sages of his time thought the moon looked like.

A century or so ago, before the advent of motion pictures, radio and television, the Jews of eastern Europe devoted enormous amounts of time to Torah study. Indeed, there were many women who were happy to marry a scholar and support him, so that he would be able to continue his studies without having to concern himself with earning a living. Some of the greatest talmudic scholars arose at that time, and in every hamlet there were people who were masters of profound biblical study. Life was physically difficult, and there was frequently the very real danger of anti-Jewish acts of violence, especially during difficult economic periods or during major Christian holidays.

And yet, despite economic hardships and the threat of mob attacks, these Jews succeeded in leading stable, happy lives; they immersed themselves in the sea of Torah and found spiritual and intellectual sustenance.

* * *

In the closing years of the twentieth century, large numbers of people, Jews and Christians, have turned away from their respective religious paths. In the wake of Hiroshima, in the aftermath of the Holocaust, and in the collapse of many moral values that followed the Vietnam debacle, people turned to secular solutions to their spiritual problems. And for many people, it simply did not work.

The case of the Soviet Jews is an excellent example of how there seems to be a deep-seated craving for genuine religious and spiritual dimensions to life. After the overthrow of the czarist regime in Russia in 1917, all religion was banned. The Soviet Union was officially atheist. The Russian Jews, whose population before the second world war was between three and four million, were ordered to throw out all vestiges of

29

Judaism. There were to be no circumcisions, no prayers, no study of Torah or Talmud or even of Hebrew, no holiday celebrations, no bar or bat mitzvahs.

From roughly 1919 until the 1970s, when the first trickle of Soviet Jews was permitted to emigrate, Judaism lay dormant in the Soviet Union. So what happened? As soon as the Soviet Jews landed in Israel or in the United States, substantial numbers sought out Jewish institutions to help them reestablish themselves as Jews. They felt a deep spiritual hunger in their hearts, they wanted their children and grandchildren to experience the study of Judaism and Torah that had been barred to them.

In Israel itself something similar happened. The early founders of the Zionist movement were largely secular Jews who had thrown off what they considered to be the shackles of the Diaspora; they equated life outside the Jewish homeland with what they called antiquated, outdated Jewish practices. So these early pioneers, filled with courage, determination and a fervent desire to create a new society based on social justice threw out practically all vestiges of Judaism, little realizing that their quest for social justice was itself an echo of biblical and prophetic teaching. The early Zionist pioneers strove to eliminate ritual laws and substitute purely ethical teachings.

Generations came and went, and again there appeared in younger Israelis a spiritual yearning. Pioneering parents were shocked when their children began to show an interest in various cults. And when a new movement began seeking to harmonize Israel's pioneering dynamism with age-old Jewish religious traditions, parents who had themselves turned away from religious practices began to return.

One of the greatest rabbis of this century, Adin Steinsaltz, who lives and works in Jerusalem, was raised to be a secularist and an atheist, but found his way to Torah study and a totally different life. Today he is a primary counselor to young Jews seeking a return to traditional Jewish religious values.

CHAPTER FOUR
THE JEWISH PEOPLE

THE THIRD OF THE THREE BASES UPON WHICH JUDAISM rests is the Jewish people; the first and second, of course, are the belief in one God and the commitment to the Torah.

There is in the Jewish community, a kind of mystique about the Jewish people. This probably stems from early in the Bible, when God in effect selects the Jews to spread His teachings. He also makes an eternal covenant with the Jewish people, something that to the best of our knowledge was not done with anyone else. Jews thus feel themselves especially fortunate because of having been chosen to carry out God's plans for the world—this does not mean that Jews feel themselves better than other peoples, worthier or wiser, but certainly different and special.

This concept of the so-called Chosen People has plagued the Jews for millenia. Anti-Semitic forces have used the term to accuse the Jews of arrogance, elitism and smug superiority. No matter how they tried, Jews could rarely explain that they were not arrogant and did not feel superior, but rather that they bore an extra, burdensome yoke. Most of their explanations fell on deaf ears.

31

Indeed, in Jewish tradition every people, every community, has a role to play in the advancement and improvement of society. In the fifth of the Five Books of Moses, the Jewish people's specific role is spelled out in sharp relief. Moses tells the ancient Israelites: "You are a holy people unto the Lord thy God; the Lord God has chosen you to be His own treasure, out of all the peoples that are on the face of the earth. The Lord did not set His love upon you nor choose you because you were more in number than any people—for you were the fewest of all peoples—but because the Lord loved you, and He would keep the oath which He swore unto your fathers . . . the Lord has brought you out with a mighty hand, and redeemed you out of the house of bondage, from the hand of Pharaoh, king of Egypt."

Thus, no matter how far they may stray from the Jewish community, no matter how little they participate in Jewish life, there remains for the overwhelming majority of Jews a faint but distinct memory that God continues to regard the Jewish people as His people, as a special community.

Whenever a disastrous situation has developed for Jews in their long history, people claim, God always seems to provide succor and support. When the large and vibrant Jewish population was summarily expelled from Spain in the fifteenth century, God guided Columbus to discover the new world, thus ensuring a future haven. When thousands of Jews were massacred in brutal pogroms in Czarist Russia in the closing years of the nineteenth century, the doors of America were thrown wide open, and hundreds of thousands of Jews streamed to the United States. And in the aftermath of the Holocaust, a modern miracle ensued—after nearly two thousand years of homelessness, a reborn Jewish state was proclaimed.

Actually, there are substantial numbers of Jews who shun the concept of the Jewish people's chosenness or specialness. A well-known rhyme (often ascribed to Dorothy Parker) says:

How odd
of God
to choose
the Jews.
To which one wit appended:
It isn't odd
The Jews
Chose God.

Perhaps one of the principal reasons for Jews to be wary of being a special or a chosen people is because this distinction carries with it certain obligations. Jews may well remember the divine admonition that accompanied the giving of the Torah at Mount Sinai. There, the Bible tells us, God said to the Israelites newly-freed from slavery: "Now therefore if you will hearken unto My voice indeed, and keep My covenant, then you shall be Mine own treasure from among all peoples; for all the earth is Mine, and you shall be unto Me a kingdom of priests, and a holy nation."

Most Jews are probably ambivalent about the whole situation: on the one hand, they feel privileged, special, chosen; on the other hand, the burden of being a holy nation, of having to constantly be wary of God looking over their shoulder, undoubtedly makes some wish that God would choose somebody else for a change. And yet, when pressed if they really feel this way, most of these Jews would probably respond, "No, I was only kidding."

Through the ages, Jewish scholars and thinkers have asked one question: why did God single out one people? Why not simply assign the task of disseminating His teachings to everybody? No fully satisfying responses have ever surfaced to this philosophical conundrum, but one explanation seems to have caught hold: that the Jews, going back to Abraham, and through the years of enslavement in Egypt, and Moses' leading them out of bondage to a new era of freedom, had—probably more than any other people—experienced God's power and His closeness. That is why God chose them; but in the end, in a perfect world, all of His peoples will share in the bounty and the peace.

One of the great rabbis of nineteenth-century Lithuania, Rabbi Nathan Finkel, interpreted the chosenness of Jews as follows: every man, Jew and non-Jew alike, is created in the image of God. A man's real character is manifested when he extends a helping hand to others, in imitation of God. People must not only help others, but must enjoy doing so. Love of others should become second nature to us.

One point must always be stressed in discussing the concept of the Jewish people and the ideas of chosenness: it does not mean that Jews are insular and interested only in their own welfare, nor does it mean that God is concerned only with the Jews. That would be a totally false interpretation. To put it another way, Judaism is both particularistic—caring deeply about what happens to the Jewish people—and at the same time universalistic, equally involved with the welfare of the world as a whole.

Indeed, rabbinical and talmudic commentators make it plain that the Torah is not meant exclusively for Jews, but is for everyone. At the same time, they note, the obligations of Judaism do not fall on Gentiles. In fact, the rabbis of the Talmud formulated a set of rules—based on passages in Genesis—that enable non-Jews to be regarded as righteous, religious people. These seven *mitzvot,* or religious commandments, are known as *Noachide* laws, for Noah was the father of all mankind, after the flood. They are:

1. All people should believe in one God and abstain from idolatry.

2. Everyone should be moral and refrain from adultery and incest.

3. People should be useful members of society and should not commit murder.

4. Everyone should be honest and refrain from stealing.

5. People should respect God and never blaspheme.

6. Law courts should be maintained to settle disputes with justice.

7. People should be kind to animals. (This apparently refers to the pagan practice of tearing the limbs from living animals, and eating them.)

Many other religions besides Judaism stress the importance of social justice, of compassion especially for the needy and downtrodden, of kindness between people. However, Judaism is aware of the fact that there are millions of people who have been brought up with values and ideas that differ totally from Jewish teaching. Jewish scholars and thinkers harbor a deep-seated tolerance for other peoples' ways of worship and prayer. There is however one bone of contention that will prevent a Jew and someone from a different faith from coming together—if that person denies the existence of one God and persists in idolatry. That is where Judaism draws the line.

There is an ingrained tradition among Jews that special concern should be paid to non-Jewish employees, friends, or neighbors. It is as though, in addition to the basic tenets taught in Judaism, Jews also recognize the fact that they are numerically a small and vulnerable people, and that if they can stand out as charitable, compassionate, concerned, chances are that their own fragile position in the world will be enhanced.

* * *

In Judaism, the memory of what transpired in past years is of vital concern today. Although events in the Bible narrative took place thousands of years ago, Jews who study the Bible may frequently feel themselves transported back to those days. More correctly, perhaps, as Jews begin to understand the characters and the weaknesses and strengths of biblical personalities, they sense that these ancients are actually living with us on earth, here and now.

An example of the presence of the past among the Jewish people is the remarkable memorial that was constructed in Jerusalem in honor of the six million Jews who perished in the

Nazi Holocaust. From all parts of the world, visitors—Jews and Gentiles—come, shed a tear or two, recall the names of the infamous death camps, and look at the photographed faces of the innocent youngsters. At the Holocaust memorial, known as Yad Vashem, trees are planted to commemorate those "righteous Gentiles" who endangered their own lives to save Jewish friends and neighbors from certain death. The bracing air of Jerusalem seems to sharpen the memory at Yad Vashem.

A visit to the Jerusalem Holocaust memorial is an experience not soon forgotten. Walking through the verdant gardens, among the trees, restores one's confidence in the essential decency of most human beings.

Even Jews whose relatives or friends were not involved in the Nazi slaughter find that when they enter the memorial they, too, are caught up in the emotional trauma of the moment. It is also not unusual to see non-Jews, visitors from many different parts of the world, break down in tears when they realize the scope and the enormity of the crime that has come to be known as the Holocaust.

Stepping out of the Yad Vashem memorial, many visitors will wipe a tear or two and then notice some young Israeli children—native-born *sabras,* as they are called—who seem to stand tall and proud. Their very appearance assures all who see them that such a calamity as the Holocaust will never recur.

* * *

There is a kind of honor system in the Jewish community that goes back many, many centuries. If a Jewish person is arrested for a crime, major or minor, fellow Jews who have never met the offender will have the same reaction. What that person has done, they will agree, is tantamount to *hilul haShem*—it is a desecration of God's name. The crime in other words embarrasses the entire Jewish community. Jews in these circumstances fear their non-Jewish neighbors will wonder

36

what kind of religion it is that turns out criminals instead of law-abiding citizens.

There is another side to this question, a concept known as *kiddush haShem*—the sanctification of God's name. This biblical phrase means that Jews bear God's name, and therefore dare not profane it. In other words, if Jews conduct themselves badly, God and the Jewish people are shamed; and if Jews produce medical breakthroughs or great works of art or whatever, then God and the Jewish people are enhanced.

Peaceful relations with all people, Jews and non-Jews, strangers and neighbors, are deemed in Judaism to be a vital component of proper behavior. Although from time to time fanatic Israeli Jews throw stones at cars being driven by Jews on the Sabbath (when driving is not permitted), it is far more common for rabbis and other observant Jews to go out of their way, on the Sabbath or on a Jewish holiday, to greet fellow Jews who are driving; they will wish each other *Shabbat Shalom* (peaceful Sabbath), or *Chag Same'ach* (happy holiday), so that friendly relations will be maintained between the religious and secular at all times.

One of the great talmudic scholars was Rabbi Johanan ben Zakai, who lived in the Holy Land some two thousand years ago. He set an example for all by greeting everyone in view, Jews and pagans alike. Indeed, the Talmud ruling could not be more explicit: Jews are required to give charity to fellow Jews in need, to visit the sick, to bury the dead, to comfort the mourners—and they are also required to do precisely the same for their non-Jewish neighbors.

* * *

Thoughtful Jews, especially in the latter years of the twentieth century when so many have received college educations, often wonder if the philosophies of other peoples are not really superior to the Jewish way of looking at life. Perhaps that is why a disproportionately large number of educated western Jews, people mostly in their twenties, go half-way around the world—to India, for example—in search of new spiritual and intellectual revelations.

This is not so unusual; throughout Jewish history there have always been people who opted to join other religious groups, explaining that they found more meaning and more relevance in their new faith than they did in Judaism. Sometimes these apostates turned into anti-Semites, and sometimes they remained emotionally attached to the Jewish community, even though they chose to live as members of another faith. There have been popes who were once Jews, as well as nuns, priests and ministers. On the other hand, there have also been Gentiles who converted to Judaism and became active, committed members and leaders of the Jewish community. In Israel today, for example, there is a bearded, Orthodox rabbi married to a woman whose parents survived the Holocaust, who is the son of a one-time Nazi official.

In the middle of the nineteenth century, the Italian Jewish scholar and philosopher Samuel D. Luzzatto wrote an essay on the differences between Judaism and Atticism, or the teachings of Athens. He said: "To Athens we owe philosophy, the arts, the sciences, the development of the intellect, order, love of beauty and grandeur, intellectual and studied morality.

"To Judaism we owe religion, the morality that springs from the heart, and from selflessness, and love of good.

"Athens is progressive, for the intellect is capable of continuous development and of new discoveries. Judaism is stationary, its teachings are immutable. The heart is capable of corruption but not of further perfection—goodness is inborn, wickedness is acquired. Judaism may rid itself of some addition alien to it, it may restore itself to its primordial condition, but it cannot be perfected.

"Athens, being progressive, takes on constantly new forms, through which it pleases, charms and attracts. Judaism, immutable, appears older and uglier every day; consequently it bores, displeases, repels. Hence the apparent dominance and triumph of the former over the latter.

"Yet, there is in human nature an inextinguishable need for the good. Beauty and grandeur cannot take the place of goodness. Society needs emotion, but intellect and Athens—far from inspiring emotion—weaken it and snuff it out. That is why human nature reacts—and always will react—in favor of the heart, of goodness, of Judaism."

On the eve of the Nazis' rise to power in Germany in 1933, Albert Einstein, already a world-acclaimed scientist, wrote a paper on Judaism and the Jewish people. He said: "Judaism appears to me to be almost exclusively concerned with the moral attitude in and toward life. Judaism [is] the content of the life-approach of the Jewish people rather than the contents of the laws laid down in the Torah and interpreted in the Talmud. Torah and Talmud are for me only the most weighty evidence of the governing concepts of Jewish life in earlier times.

"The essence of the Jewish concept of life seems to be the affirmation of life for all creatures. For the life of the individual has meaning only in the service of enhancing and ennobling the life of every living thing. Life is holy, i.e., it is the highest worth on which all other values depend. The sanctification of the life which transcends the individual brings with it reverence for the spiritual, a peculiarly characteristic trait of Jewish tradition.

"Judaism is not a faith. The Jewish God is but a negation of superstition and an imaginative result of its elimination. He also represents an attempt to ground morality in fear—a deplorable, discreditable attempt. Yet it seems to me that the powerful moral tradition in the Jewish people has, in great measure, released itself from this fear. Moreover, it is clear that 'to serve God' is equivalent to serving 'every living thing.' It is for this that the best among the Jewish people ceaselessly battled. Thus Judaism is not a transcendental religion—it is concerned only with the tangible experiences of life, and with nothing else. Therefore it seems to me to be questionable whether it may be termed a 'religion' in the customary sense of the word, especially since no 'creed' is demanded of Jews, but only the sanctification of life in its all-inclusive sense.

"There remains however something else in the Jewish tradition, so gloriously revealed in certain of the Psalms, namely, a kind of drunken joy and surprise at the beauty and incomprehensible sublimity of this world, of which man can attain but a faint intimation. It is the feeling from which genuine research draws its intellectual strength, but also seems to manifest itself in the song of birds. This appears to me to be the loftiest content of the God-idea.

"Is this then the characteristic of Judaism? And does it exist elsewhere under other names? In pure form it exists nowhere, not even in Judaism where too much literalism obscures the pure doctrine. Nevertheless, I see in Judaism one of its most vital and pure realizations. This is especially true of its fundamental principle of the sanctification of life.

"In the commandment to keep the Sabbath holy the animals were also expressly included. Far more strongly is expressed the demand for the solidarity of all humankind; and it is no accident that the socialist demands emanated for the most part from Jews.

"How great an extent the consciousness of the sanctity of life is alive in the Jewish people is expressed by a remark of Walter Rathenau. He said, When a Jew says he takes pleasure in the hunt, he lies. It is impossible to illustrate more poignantly the consciousness of the sanctity and unity of all life as it exists in the Jewish people."

CHAPTER FIVE

ISRAEL AND JUDAISM

ALTHOUGH MOST RABBIS AND JEWISH SCHOLARS WILL agree that Judaism rests on a three-part base comprised of belief in one God, devotion to and faith in the Torah, and commitment to Jewish peoplehood, there is an additional factor, one that has received special attention in this century, that has a powerful bearing and impact on Jews: the unique place of Israel in the hearts and minds of the overwhelming majority of the Jewish people.

In a memorable phrase, the comedian Alan King summed it up very well when he said that he loved the United States because she was like his wife, and at the same time he loved Israel, for she was like his mother. Most Jews can relate to that.

To fully understand the special situation that Israel occupies in the consciousness of Jews, one has to go back to the early years of the twentieth century. World War I began in 1914, and was fought initially between Germany (and Ottoman Turkey) on one side, and England, France, and later Russia,

41

on the other. The United States entered the war late in 1917 to aid England and France, and at the same time to help the Russian regime.

Many American Jews, newly-arrived immigrants and those who had been in the United States longer, held the Russians in such contempt for their virulent anti-Semitic pogroms that they campaigned for the United States not to join in the allied war effort. These Jews actually preferred that the Germans win, rather than help bolster the hated czarist regime.

The overwhelming majority of Jewish immigrants to the United States were refugees escaping from persecution and discrimination; they turned their backs on their hated former homelands and looked upon America as the Golden Land, the nation that glorified freedom and equality, where a person was judged on his own merits and not by his religion, color or ethnic origin. And in the early years of the twentieth century, the Jews who had reached America threw themselves into becoming full-fledged Americans, as rapidly and as totally as possible.

For many, religious observance became secondary. The nascent Zionist movement, that had been launched by Theodor Herzl and fellow Europeans in 1897 at the first World Zionist Congress, drew a very weak response from the Jewish community in America.

Slowly, however, a new perception of the need for a Jewish homeland developed in the American Jewish community. In 1917, when the then mighty British Empire issued the Balfour Declaration pledging to the Jewish people the eventual establishment of a Jewish homeland in Palestine, American Jews began to take notice of the events that were unfolding at that ancient site on the eastern shores of the Mediterranean.

In the 1920s and 1930s, American Jews also became aware of other factors: many of their fellow immigrants, people who came from Ireland, or Italy, or Sweden, or elsewhere, spoke of their former homelands with pride and nostalgia; the Jews found themselves mute at these moments, for in almost all cases they had been forced to flee not so much for better economic opportunities as for their very lives. They missed being able to reminisce about the old country. Many began to cast their eyes toward Palestine, which was gradually beginning to acquire a sizable Jewish population.

In the decade of the thirties, two disasters made Jews realize even more sharply how vulnerable they were, and how a Jewish state—especially for those coreligionists in desperate need—really mattered. First, the 1929 financial crash and the resulting economic depression in America hit home with a vengeance, and the tense atmosphere that enveloped the whole of the country worried many Jews. And then in 1933, when the Nazis came to power in Germany and their supporters in the United States, England, France and other countries began to emulate the Nazis' anti-Semitism, Jews began to realize how powerless they were, and again more and more of them looked toward the Promised Land for potential support and even refuge.

In the years between the Nazis' rise to power and the onset of World War II in September 1939, very few countries offered sanctuary to the endangered Jews of Germany, Austria and Czechoslovakia—except the Jewish community in Palestine. Had there been, in those years, an independent Jewish state, many more European Jews could have been saved during the Holocaust.

Thus, even before the establishment of Israel in May 1948, deep feeling for the nascent Jewish state gradually developed among Jews in all parts of the world. In the 1940s and 1950s, this pro-Israel sentiment grew so strong among American Jews—particularly when Israel threw open its gates and admitted hundreds of thousands of survivors of the Naxi camps as well as impoverished and oppressed Jews of the Arab world—that a few Jews feared they would be accused of "dual loyalty." To demonstrate that they were Americans first, last and always, and that they had no political or even emotional links with Israel, this peripheral group formed an organization

43

called the American Council for Judaism. It lasted for a few years, attracting minuscule numbers, and eventually all but disappeared; the overwhelming majority of Jews, religious and secular, rich and poor, socialist or capitalist, became profoundly attached to Israel. Indeed, prayers composed in recent years talk of the rebirth of Israel as the "beginning of the Jewish people's redemption."

For a large number of Jews, Israel has become a vital, central part of Jewish life. The Israeli-style Sephardic pronunciation of Hebrew has all but replaced the older Ashkenazic accent. Synagogue services have incorporated Israeli melodies; rabbinical sermons frequently discuss Israel. Approximately one million American Jews have visited Israel, and many have returned for second and third trips. There are numerous summer programs for teens and college students in Israel, attracting thousands of youths. They provide a rare opportunity for American Jews to meet with, and get to know, coreligionists from practically every part of the world.

The world Jewish community probably did not itself realize how deep was its attachment to Israel until the fateful days that preceded the June 1967 Six-Day War. It was a time when nothing less than a second Holocaust loomed for the Jewish community of Israel, and the unprecedented outpouring of financial and emotional support that immediately preceded the fighting amazed Jews, Israelis, and the world at large.

It was as though the Jews of 1967 still felt guilty that they had not fought like lions to rescue their coreligionists from their Nazi captors, and were now determined that such a calamity would not be allowed to recur. And then, when the Israelis, through skillful military operations, managed to defeat Egypt, Syria and Jordan in a swift six-day assault, Jews throughout the world felt vindicated—the courage and fighting abilities of the Israelis filled every Jew in the world with vicarious pride. The wheel had finally turned full circle: the biblical tales of Maccabean courage, which had been blurred by two millenia of ghetto subjugation, had reappeared, only now the heroes were the young Jews wearing the uniforms of the Israel Defense Force. In the final years of the twentieth century, the Jewish people's feelings for Israel have grown even more rooted. They note with pride and gratification that all Jews in need and distress now turn to Israel and find haven there. They regard the relocation of a vast number of Soviet Jews to the Jewish state as a modern miracle, for these people were cruelly severed from the world's Jewish community for more than seventy years. Israel, Jews know, is the only Jewish community in the world with a growing Jewish population, resulting both from a steady stream of immigration and from what is euphemistically referred to as "internal immigration"—its high birth rate. Israel today is already the second largest Jewish community in the world, and many demographers believe that it will even surpass the United States in a couple of generations.

There is in the Jewish community today a feeling that Israel is the "old country," just as Ireland, Italy, and other countries are for non-Jewish Americans. Jews even smile a little nowadays when they hear of an anti-Semitic demonstration in which Jews are told to "go back" to Israel. A half-century ago there was no place for them to go home to.

By and large most Jews look upon Israel with enormous pride, respect and admiration. Jews in South Africa, England, various European and Latin American countries, and to a lesser degree America, have begun to settle or retire in Israel, or to maintain a second home there. Being a Jew in Israel, these people explain, is easy—not only is there no anti-Semitism, but the parents of young children are free from the ever-present threat of intermarriage and defection from Judaism. It is also, for many Jews, a unique experience to live in a community where Jews are the majority; many Jewish immigrants or visitors from the west say that when they are in Israel they shed the psychological yokes that they have been carrying—often unknowingly—and they feel lighter and more relaxed.

Thus, as Jews in western countries see Israel absorbing

45

more and more Jews in distress (and thus bolstering the
ancient concept of Jewish peoplehood), and as they note the
proliferation of Jewish scholarly pursuits in Israel (in tribute
to the principle of Torah study and observance), they begin to
realize that Israel has, over the years, come to be more and
more woven into the fabric of Judaism. Many Jews understand, of course, that belief in one God is still the first and
basic principle of Jewish belief, and they now have equivocal
views on this: on the one hand they see yarmulke-wearing,
tough-looking young Israeli soldiers, and they marvel at, perhaps even envy them, their faith; and on the other hand, there
is a feeling that faith in one God will follow if one studies
Torah seriously and commits oneself to the well-being of the
Jewish people.

* * *

On a superficial level, one can say that Jewish religious
observances in Israel and abroad are broadly similar. Approximately 15 percent of the Jews in Israel and a similar number in
the U.S., for example, may be considered "religious," i.e., they
maintain a kosher home, attend Sabbath and holiday services
regularly, devote a certain amount of time to Torah study, and
take an active interest in Jewish religious/educational/cultural
life.

In Israel, however, there is one significant difference. The
official day of rest for the whole country is the Jewish Sabbath,
Saturday. The national holidays celebrated are taken from the
Jewish calendar; during the High Holy Days, radio and television broadcast suitable liturgical music. The big weekend papers appear on Fridays, and no papers are published on
Saturday. And even the most irreligious Israeli Jews greet each
other on the Sabbath with the lovely phrase, *Shabbat Shalom,*
or peaceful Sabbath.

A friend of the writer is an executive in the toy industry. He
has both Jewish and Gentile friends and lives in a New York
suburb. Each year he visits Israel, where he dons a yarmulke

and never takes it off for the entire two or three weeks of his stay. Laughingly, he explains, "I just like it—it feels right."

There is a mystique about the Land of Israel in Judaism. The great Medieval biblical commentator Nahmanides said that "the Torah cannot assume perfection, except in Israel." The famed Hassidic master Nachman of Bratislav taught that "no matter where I go, it is always to Israel."

Jews are aware of biblical promises and prophecy that state unequivocally that God will restore the Jews to their ancient homeland. For many Jews this creates ambivalent feelings: on the one hand, most American Jews, for example, feel themselves deeply rooted, in every possible way, in the United States, and they acknowledge Israel as a heaven-sent haven for Jews in need, but not for them; yet, on the other hand, all around them they see a growing intermarriage rate, with the resulting assimilation of Jews into the majority culture, and a gradual erosion of the Jewish community. They are also—in their heart of hearts—troubled about the possibilities of serious anti-Semitic outbreaks in the United States.

In recent years, anti-Jewish incidents have escalated in America on the part of certain elements in the Black community, on the part of racist neo-Nazi groups, and even on American college campuses. Older American Jews remember vividly the hate-filled marchers of the pro-Hitler organizations; younger American Jews are more puzzled by the sporadic outbursts of anti-Jewish violence and sentiments.

For all these people, Israel represents a positive option, a beacon of hope, a small country fully deserving of support and strengthening. This of course does not mean that American Jews are not fully committed to America; they are, indeed, very much so, for many reasons, including one special reason—American Jews wish to see the U.S. and Israel forge closer ties and become full-fledged allies. Only one percent of U.S. Jews, some 60,000 people, have emigrated from the U.S. and established permanent domicile in Israel, and most of these have retained their American citizenship, opting to be

47

dual citizens of the U.S. and of Israel. Whether that percentage will grow in coming years depends largely on external factors: assimilation's threat, possible anti-Semitism, or possibly a new, reinvigorated desire to live a more Jewish life in a Jewish majority.

Ingrained in the consciousness of many Jews, in all parts of the world, sensed if not actually known, are the ancient prophetic words of Isaiah: "He will assemble the dispersed of Israel . . . the Lord will set them in their own land . . . the Lord binds up the bruise of His people."

Jews are profoundly aware of the Law of Return, one of the first pieces of legislation passed by Israel's Knesset (parliament) two years after the country's independence was proclaimed. "Every Jew," the law says, "has the right to immigrate to Israel," and automatically becomes an Israeli citizen. Jews are also aware of Israel's Declaration of Independence, which stated: "The Land of Israel was the birthplace of the Jewish people. Here their spiritual, religious and national identity was formed. Here they achieved independence and created a culture of national and universal significance. . . . Impelled by this historic association, Jews strove throughout the centuries to go back to the land of their fathers and regain their statehood."

The architect and first prime minister of Israel, David Ben Gurion, summed up in a 1949 statement what Israel should become: "The State of Israel will prove itself not by material wealth, not by military might or technical achievement, but by its moral character and human values." Thus, Jews look upon Israel as an innate, ongoing expression of Judaism's highest moral teachings. Indeed, in the closing years of the twentieth century, and in recognition of Israel's nearly half-century of independence, it is safe to say that, deep in their hearts, Jews today see Judaism as composed of four elements—belief in one God, Torah study and observance, commitment to Jewish peoplehood, and an unshakable love for Israel.

* * *

There are many rabbis who see in the restoration of Israel the beginning of the long-promised messianic age. Most of those inclined to this mystical interpretation of Jewish history qualify their remarks by stating that it is only the beginning, a gradual dawning of what is to come. The usual explanation for this qualification is that Israel itself is not yet redeemed nor of course is the rest of the world, and yet, Israel should not be looked upon solely as a secular community, but rather as a special nation that already has elements of messianic redemption.

Religious life and institutions in Israel differ in many respects from Jewish life in other countries. For one thing, although there are a small number of Reform and Conservative synagogues in Israel, the great majority of Israel's thousands of houses of worship are strictly orthodox, and they have traditionally opposed changes in worship or observance that have been incorporated into most western synagogues. Unfortunately this has resulted in sharp controversies between religious and secular Jews, and among various religious groupings.

American and other western Jews, visiting Israel or living there for longer periods of time, have either had to compromise and accept an Orthodox mode of prayer, or have sought out synagogues where the prayer services and general ambience remind them more nearly of their home communities.

There are other religious problems peculiar to Israel. A Ministry of Religion supervises synagogues, churches and mosques. This results in some odd situations: only orthodox rabbis can perform Jewish weddings that are recognized by the state; if, however, a married couple comes to Israel, no one questions who married them. What generally happens is that young Israeli couples, therefore, who may be totally secular, are married by traditional, orthodox rabbis; while those who reject such a ceremony get around the law by getting married abroad either by a Reform or a Conservative rabbi, or in a civil ceremony.

There are other religious situations that are peculiar to modern Israel. The country's two major political parties, Likud and Labor, often have to form coalition governments with smaller, but crucially important, religious parties. These in turn, as payment for their collaboration, make certain religious demands which are usually met, despite the opposition of large sections of the population.

Thus, there is no public transport on the Sabbath in Jerusalem, Tel Aviv, or most Israeli cities. Secular Jews who often work six days a week (Sundays through Friday), and who are not able to own a private car, feel themselves discriminated against since they are not able to go anywhere on their one Sabbath day of rest.

* * *

The first president of Israel, Chaim Weizmann, an eminent chemist, used to say that he dreamt of the day when Israel would become the Switzerland of the Middle East. Strangely enough, that is not so far-fetched as it may have sounded a half-century ago. Israel is today still a small country and poor in natural resources. Long ago it came to realize that its best hope for economic survival, and for peace and prosperity, lay in developing a highly-skilled, technologically-advanced industrial base that would depend primarily on brainpower. Slowly, Israel has been advancing this concept and is already a major producer of medical and other scientific devices and components. Most Jews long for the day when Israel will be able to trade peacefully with its neighbors, exchanging its scientific skills for products in which the Arab states are rich.

And for most Jews around the world an additional phrase continues to reverberate, an ancient line repeated every Sabbath in the synagogue: "From Zion shall come forth the Torah."

CHAPTER SIX
JUDAISM AND FAMILY

TH HEBREW WORD *MISHPACHAH*—FAMILY—APPEARS FRE-
quently in the Bible. The family is the basic, nuclear unit of the
Jewish people. And the entire Jewish people itself is considered by many as one big family. Sometimes there are family
disputes, but more often there is cohesion, caring, commitment. Visitors to Israel often express their awe at how Israelis
interact with one another, as a vast group.

A number of years ago a leading New York City bank
advertised that "you have a friend" at the bank—to which a
competing Israeli bank responded, "but at our bank you have
family."

For many centuries the Jewish community fostered a special
phenomenon known as *yichus,* best translated as family pride.
To a lesser extent this factor still exists, particularly in the
Hassidic and ultra-Orthodox sectors. When a child married,
the partnership was usually arranged by the parents, or at least
the parents were consulted. And more often than not, one of
the factors in the equation which determined whether or not it

was going to be a good match was yichus: specifically, was the bride or groom descended from a line of rabbis, scholars, communal leaders?

For most parents in modern Jewish families, yichus is a thing of the past; if the family of the intended spouse can be described as "nice," or "good Jews," or "kind people," that generally suffices. As a result, a growing number of Jewish families have unusual backgrounds—second marriages, adoptive parents, half-siblings, converts to Judaism, unaffiliated non-practicing Jews.

Nevertheless, one can still find great emphasis placed on yichus in certain Orthodox communities in Brooklyn, New York and Jerusalem, where wedding announcements in the local papers will report that the son of one revered rabbi will soon marry the daughter of another famed rabbi.

* * *

Gentiles sometimes find it difficult to understand why Jewish parents are so adamantly opposed to their children marrying non-Jews. Gentile parents frequently take umbrage: in effect they ask, isn't our son or daughter good enough, nice enough, for you? Why are you so antagonistic?

Their reaction is understandable, but in actuality they do not understand. There are of course many "intermarriages" within other communities, between a Catholic and a Protestant, between someone of Irish ancestry and someone of Italian ethnicity. A marriage between a Gentile and a Jewish young person, however, is very different.

One first has to understand the background of Jewish families. They have always seen themselves as a minority, and there has always been an instinctive desire to preserve that minority. In pre-World War II Poland, the Jewish community comprised nearly ten percent of the population, but in the United States today Jews represent only two and a half percent of the whole. There is a gut feeling that marriages with non-Jews will very soon cut that figure drastically.

Then there is the Holocaust factor. Many Jews, even those who are proudly unobservant, refuse to give Hitler what they call a posthumous victory—intermarriage and assimilation eventually leading to the disappearance of the Jewish community. There is a feeling that somehow Jews managed to survive the Nazis, to begin to rebuild their numbers, and now, ironically through the joyousness of a wedding, Jews will again suffer losses in number and identity.

There is still another factor operating here: most Jews, religious or irreligious, take pride in their heritage. They sense that Jews have made outstanding contributions to society, and will continue to do so; they also feel the strong pull of the long chain of Jewish history, from biblical times to today, a chain in which every link is vital. They genuinely believe that being Jewish, leading a Jewish life, being a member of the Jewish community—despite anti-Semitism, despite special problems that Jews often have to face—is all worthwhile. Perhaps it is an almost tribal instinct which stretches back to Mount Sinai; perhaps it is stubbornness, determination and an unwillingness to give up a heritage prized by parents, grandparents, family, friends—the idea of a Jewish child opting to marry outside the community and turn his or her back on Judaism produces great pain and resentment.

On the other hand, when a Gentile partner agrees to convert to Judaism, more often than not the Jewish family into which he or she is marrying will be fully accepting, and will treat the convert not only as a full-fledged Jew, but as someone very special who has chosen to assume the burdens of a minority faith. (Actually, according to Jewish law, no one who converts to Judaism because he or she wishes to marry a Jew should be accepted—the only reason a person should be accepted as a convert is because he or she, after a suitable course of study and contemplation, has decided that Judaism is more rewarding, more fulfilling and more acceptable. Of course, in real life it doesn't usually work that way; but when a sincere young Christian expresses a desire to convert because of a deep respect for Judaism, most rabbis will shy away from asking if there is a prospective marriage to a Jew on the horizon).

One other aspect of conversion to Judaism that is sometimes overlooked is the reaction of the convert's family to the Jewish family and to Judaism. There are cases of the parents being happy when their child opts to convert and marry a Jew, and there are also cases where the opposite holds true. For a sizable number of Gentile families, a child's decision to become Jewish produces a backlash of bitterness and resentment.

A century ago, in Eastern Europe, where the bulk of the world's Jews lived at the time, intermarriage between a Jew and a Gentile was a rare occurrence. When it did take place, it was generally a Jew who married a Christian, and agreed to convert to Christianity. This usually resulted in the Jewish parents considering their child as dead, and actually reciting the mourner's prayers for their offspring. In those days, it was even rarer for a Christian to convert to Judaism, so that at the time that particular problem did not arise.

Nowadays, in the United States and other western countries, the situation is totally different from a century or even sixty years ago. A very large percentage of Jewish youths attend college, often out of town, where—frequently for the first time—they are exposed to a new world of non-Jewish classmates, both male and female. They are at an age when rebelliousness against parental authority is almost second nature. They also see that superficially at least there are no real major differences between themselves and their Gentile friends. Friendships blossom into romances, young people fall in love, and soon there is another possible intermarriage in the offing.

There is a school of thought that believes that Jewish men are often attracted to Gentile women as potential spouses because "opposites attract." Perhaps that is true. There is also a view that says many Jewish men who choose to marry Gentile women do so because, subconsciously at least, that will root them ever more deeply into American society. By such a marriage, the theory goes, these particular men will move from the two and a half percent Jewish minority to the ninety-seven and a half percent majority.

There is still another factor at work in this complex situation. Jewish husbands, fairly or otherwise, have gotten a reputation for being exceptionaly good—they are, it is said, excellent providers, like to spoil their wives with elaborate gifts, do not drink or beat their wives, and make excellent fathers. How accurate this is remains a moot question, but one can begin to understand the dilemma of a young Jewish man who meets a pretty young Gentile girl who believes he is the one man in the universe she wants, and sets her cap for him, as the saying goes.

* * *

In Judaism, marriage is not only a sacred institution, as it is for many other religious groups, but it is also analogous to the "marriage" between God and the Jewish people. Many of the ancient prophets refer to that special relationship as a loving, monogamous marriage.

Judaism teaches that everyone should get married, that they should do so at an early age (the Bible speaks of eighteen as a suitable age for a groom), and that they should "be fruitful and multiply."

When a man meets the right woman in marriage, the Talmud teaches, he has found goodness. Although Judaism permits divorce, it stresses the care that should be taken to make marriage a joyous relationship. In ancient times, Jewish men were permitted to have more than one wife, a stipulation that was rescinded more than a thousand years ago; most rabbis explain that even in biblical times, monogamy was the ideal, and permission for additional wives grew out of the fact that in those days a woman who lived alone, without male protection, was in grave peril.

Judaism does not sanction a monastic, ascetic life; there are no Jewish monks or nuns, and sexual union between husband and wife is looked upon not only as an act of procreation but also as an expression of love and joy. Traditionally, for example, on the eve of Sabbath, after a festive meal replete with religious songs and sealed by the recital of grace, a Jewish couple is encouraged to crown their celebration by sexual union.

Already in the early part of Genesis, where we first encounter Adam, we hear God declaring that "it is not good that the man should be alone, I will make him a helpmate against him." To which a talmudic commentator centuries later said: "If he is worthy, she is a helpmate; if he is unworthy, she is against him."

There has thus been, from biblical times, a strong tradition on behalf of marriage and family. The great Rabbi Akiba wrote: "He who is unmarried impairs the divine image." Hiyya ben Gamada taught that "without a wife, a man is incomplete." And in the Zohar, the basic text of Jewish mysticism, it is taught that "a man is not even called a man till he is united with a woman," and "an unmarried man is deficient and blemished."

In the Talmud, where an entire tractate *(Kiddushin)* is devoted to marriage and family, one rabbi advises: "Whoever marries for money will have unworthy children." A Hassidic text states: "A youth need not obey his parents if they urge him to marry not the girl he loves but another with money." The same source declares: "Marry into a family of pure, kind and honorable proselytes rather than into a family of Jews who lack these qualities."

* * *

A Jewish wedding ceremony is a beautiful, spiritually significant event. The young couple stands, usually with their parents and sometimes also with grandparents, under a canopy known as a *chupah*. The ceremony is often held in the synagogue, in front of the Holy Ark that houses the scrolls of the Torah. The rabbi, sometimes aided by a cantor, faces the young couple, reads to them from the ancient marriage contract *(ketubah)*. He recites a blessing over wine and adds a special blessing praising God for sanctifying the Jewish people through the institution of marriage, and the wine is shared by the couple. The rabbi then leads the groom in the recitation of the ancient words: "Be thou consecrated unto me with this ring, according to the law of Moses and Israel." The groom places a gold ring on the bride's index finger (and in some ceremonies the bride now places a ring on her future husband's finger). At this point the rabbi will often interject a few words, reminding the young couple of the importance of maintaining a Jewish home where love and tranquility will prevail; if the rabbi is an old family friend, he might speak of the years he has known the bride or the groom, and comment on their lifelong devotion to Judaism.

The ketubah that the groom hands his wife is an ancient legal document, written in Aramaic, in which he promises to support her and take care of her, and that, in the event of a divorce or his predeceasing her, he will continue to provide for her. In addition to the authority of this Jewish marriage contract, rabbis officiate in accordance with the civil laws of the particular state in which they reside.

After the reading of the ketubah, the cantor (or rabbi) chants the traditional *sheva b'rachot* (seven blessings), which speak of joy, delight, happiness, a groom and bride's love for one another, and God's placing of Adam and Eve in the Garden of Eden.

Immediately after this, the young couple take another sip of wine from their common goblet.

Then comes the explosive moment when the groom is asked to stomp on a glass on the floor, symbolizing the fact that, even at this most joyous of moments, we must always remember the destruction of the Holy Temple in Jerusalem. The implication here is that the newlyweds will join the rest of the Jewish people in bolstering the Jewish community, so that some day in the far-off future the temple will be rebuilt, and Jerusalem will again become a city of peace and faith.

The moment the glass smashes, everyone in the wedding party shouts *mazel tov,* the groom finally embraces and kisses his wife, and everyone goes off to dance, sing, eat and be merry.

* * *

The rhythm of Jewish family life is not difficult to follow. After a couple is married and they have established a home and working lives, parents in particular and people in general will begin to ask the one-word question: *"Nu?"* Translation: *Well,* when do you have children? Judaism regards couples that are capable of having children, and do not do so as neglecting a major *mitzvah,* or commandment, of life. Couples who cannot have children are encouraged either to adopt a needy child, or to try the newest methods of birth stimulation.

Ancient rabbis like Hillel taught that every family should have at least two children, a boy and a girl. Among some ultra-Orthodox Jews there is a belief that every couple should now strive for twelve children, both in memory of the twelve tribes of Israel, and as a response to the Nazis' attempt to wipe out the Jewish people.

Of course, bringing children into the world means assuming a great responsibility. Judaism teaches that parents must provide a happy home for their children, where the youngsters can develop healthily, in mind and body. Children must also be educated, both in secular knowledge and in Jewish religious learning; one talmudic rabbi argues that a father who does not enable his son to learn a vocation so that he can earn a living is, in a sense, rearing that child to become a criminal.

Jewish male children, in accordance with biblical command, are circumcised at the age of eight days. At the same time they are given their Jewish names. (An infant girl is usually named in a simple synagogue ceremony, a few weeks after her birth).

The *Brit Mila,* or circumcision ceremony, is explained in the Bible as indicating the covenant that exists between God and the Jewish people. Some biblical commentators explain the circumcision ceremony as a sign that God wanted to show that man must join Him in perfecting the world—just as a small boy needs help on entering the world by removing his foreskin, so we must work to help God by continually seeking to improve the world around us. That is, God expects people to be His partners in creating a better world.

Many people are aware of the Bar Mitzvah ceremony for boys and Bat Mitzvah for girls. Although these are now very popular events in all Jewish communities, they did not actually evolve until the Middle Ages. *Bar Mitzvah* means a "son of the commandment," someone (a boy at thirteen, a girl usually at twelve) who is now old enough, and presumably mature enough, to take on themselves responsibility for the commandments of Judaism, and thus relieve their parents from bearing it on their behalf. In most synagogues, the ceremony consists of a youngster reading from a special Sabbath Torah portion in a traditional chant that often takes weeks or months to learn. The reception that follows the ceremony tends, one wit has noted, to accentuate the "bar" rather than the "mitzvah."

Judaism warns parents not to be too easygoing in rearing their children, lest they turn out spoiled and unfit for coping with life. On the other hand, Judaism also teaches that children have certain obligations to their parents: The fifth of the Ten Commandments states explicitly: "Honor thy father and thy mother," and then adds, "so that thy days may be long." The usual explanation of the second phrase is that children who appreciate life will respect their parents and will also look upon life in general as a divine blessing.

Regretably, there are some children who retort early in their lives, in deed if not in word: "Why should I honor my parents? I didn't ask to be born. That was their decision." This

is a very anti-Jewish viewpoint; notwithstanding all the difficulties and problems that confront people, Judaism believes
that life is good, worth living and struggling for, and that in
general we should help others, strive to enjoy life's bounty,
and try to leave this world a little better than when we first
arrived on the scene.

The Jewish family is a unit that is "one for all, and all for
one." Parents are expected to be totally committed to their
children's welfare and vice versa. Indeed, there is a special
word in Yiddish and Hebrew that is almost untranslatable,
naches—in essence parental joy, the special satisfaction that
parents feel when they conclude that their children have
turned out to be upstanding citizens, contributing and caring
members of society, and at the same time active and devoted
members of the Jewish community. It is not so unusual for a
low-income Jewish parent to announce: "I'm rich! I have lots
of naches!"

It is interesting to note that the talmudic sages and rabbis of
old were way ahead of their time. Centuries ago, they interpreted the commandment about honoring one's father and
mother very liberally. The rabbis taught, and still do today,
that if parents tell a child to do something that he considers
wrong, he is to disobey. Parents are advised to understand that
children have rights, just as they do, and the best way to
resolve issues is through tact and gentleness.

Judaism also urges all people to respect not only their
parents, but virtually anyone of advanced years, even an atheist, for that person may well have learned many of life's truths.
Special emphasis is also placed on respecting one's teachers,
who are referred to as parents in the sense that they, too, help
to shape our characters.

In the Jewish view, learning is a lifelong, ongoing activity,
and is the result of two separate inputs—study, and life's
experiences; learning is, moreover, never to be regarded as a
single, granite-like block, but rather as an ever-evolving, ever-

changing adventure, in which we grow and mature together with our new comprehensions.

A Jewish home, traditionally, must be a warm, friendly and hospitable place, where love, wisdom, joy and hope prevail. Substitute the word "family" for "home", and that is Judaism's ideal family.

CHAPTER SEVEN
BASIC BELIEFS

ONE OF THE MOST DIFFICULT MOMENTS THAT JEWISH adults face is when their children ask them questions such as, What is Judaism? What does it mean to be Jewish? Can you be Jewish and not be religious? Do all Jews have the same beliefs, follow the same commandments?

It is hard for adult Jews, including those who have devoted a certain amount of time to serious study of the Jewish texts, to respond to those questions. Scholars, rabbis, great teachers have all tried, and many have even attempted to codify rules and regulations in order to enable Jews to lead acceptable Jewish lives wherever they might be. The "Thirteen Principles of Faith" composed by Maimonides set out to explain Judaism philosophically, and through the centuries they surely must have helped many Jews reach a better understanding of Judaism.

In the sixteenth century a great Jewish scholar in central Europe, Joseph Caro, wrote the *Shulchan Aruch,* a compilation of all the religious laws and observances that Jews had known up to that time. For many Orthodox Jews the work remains a code and guide to practice to this day.

Thus, through the years there have been many attempts to detail the philosophical beliefs of Judaism as well as the ritual observances, for it was recognized that each approach complements the other in a harmonious, fulfilling Jewish life.

In his seminal work *Basic Judaism* the late Rabbi Milton Steinberg admitted that summarizing the fundamental principles of Judaism was "far from simple." Nonetheless, he made an effort to do so. Judaism, he taught, is like a torch in which seven strands are interwoven: 1. A basic belief about God and man; 2. Moral teachings for society and for each individual; 3. A disciplined code of customs, ceremonies and rituals; 4. A legal doctrine; 5. A hallowed literature; 6. Institutions through which the aforementioned are developed and maintained; 7. The central role of Jewish peoplehood as a component of Judaism.

Like the late, great Rabbi Mordecai Kaplan who taught that "Judaism is a civilization," Steinberg believed that "Judaism is an organism" that is alive, vital and subject to change and growth.

And like Abraham Joshua Heschel, Steinberg also emphasized the key importance of the time factor in Judaism. With a heritage stretching back some four thousand years, Judaism tends to look at human problems from the perspective that "there is nothing new under the sun." Human nature, Judaism teaches, has not really changed in all those long years. Human strengths and weaknesses, human spiritual needs, human hunger for fulfillment, for a link to eternal life, all these have remained more or less constant. Forms, outward manifestations, appearances, all these may change, but the hard-core ways and needs of people, their very substance, do not.

True, there are those who even question whether it is possible to enumerate the basic beliefs of Judaism, a religion or a religious way of life that has taken so many thousands of years to evolve, and in which so many people have contributed thoughts, concepts and comments. It is as though Judaism were born as an infant, grew up, matured, reached adulthood, and attained the hoary years—can that older person still be compared to the small child?

Has there been a steady, unchanging pattern of behavior and beliefs that has characterized Jewish life throughout the years? The answer is a strong affirmative. Despite many historical permutations, interpretations, vicissitudes, Judaism has remained the same—like most religions, dedicated to a higher ethical standard, and in its own unique way, challenging its adherents to achieve a higher moral plateau through deeds as well as through rational, intellectual study.

* * *

Above the Holy Ark in most synagogues, where the scrolls of the Torah are generally housed, there appears a biblical quotation: "Love your neighbor as yourself." Certainly a beautiful, compassionate phrase, but, some Jewish philosophers ask, how realistic is it? Is it always or even sometimes possible to love our neighbors as ourselves?

Judaism has always sought to present itself to the Jewish people as a practical, livable and do-able religion. If this particular command from Leviticus is to be followed seriously, then it requires a certain amount of discussion and understanding. After all, to be fair, if someone wishes to follow Judaism's teachings fully, and yet his neighbor happens to be a mean, selfish, awful person, why should he torment himself into loving him when his common sense tells him to avoid him like the plague?

Commentators correctly explain that this verse has been taken out of context, and that the full text really teaches: "You shall not take vengeance, nor bear any grudge against the children of your people, but you shall love your neighbor as yourself; I am the Lord." That little word "but" makes all the difference: the verse really says, do not practice revenge, do not try to get even for a wrong done to you, but rather try to behave as if nothing wrong had been done to you, and as you would like your neighbor to behave toward you.

The lesson of this verse then is deed, rather than creed. By a person's movement toward kindness, rather than such negative attitudes like revenge or bearing a grudge, a person can rise to new moral heights.

By and large, Judaism takes a hopeful slant on people and on life. Good deeds, kind actions, compassionate behavior, all these can, in the course of time, transform weak or selfish characters into better people. Judaism essentially believes that people are born with two conflicting inclinations—the evil and the good. Throughout life, it is felt, people struggle between both drives, and sometimes one wins out and sometimes the other. And one sure way to achieve more victories for the good inclination is to retrain oneself, as it were, to perform acts of kindness that will in time become second nature, and thus weaken and outweigh the evil drive that always lurks within.

* * *

"L'chaim!", To Life! is the traditional Jewish toast. Life is the single holiest factor in Judaism. The talmudic rabbis teach that "he who saves one life, it is as though he has saved a whole world." On the obverse of that same coin, Jews are taught that "whoever destroys a single human life, it is as if he had destroyed a whole world." This fundamental teaching of Judaism applies of course to all people, for Judaism believes strongly that everyone is a child of God.

There are talmudic discussions as to what is the proper procedure if two men are walking through the desert with one bottle of water between them—enough to sustain one of them, but not both. Should one give up the bottle for the sake of the other? Should they share it for a time, knowing that in the end both would die? There are strong arguments on both sides of the case, with no definitive resolution, except a general ruling that nobody in such a situation can determine whose life is more important or of greater value.

In its supreme reverence for life, Judaism teaches that almost anything can be done to preserve life—the Sabbath may be violated, non-kosher food may be consumed, lies may be told. There are, however, three situations in which death is preferable to life: nobody may commit murder, nobody may worship pagan idols, and nobody may indulge in incest or adultery. Outside of these, Judaism teaches that life may, and indeed must, be defended valiantly and fully.

A talmudic tale of the fourth century tells of a Jew who was ordered by a tyrannical leader in ancient Babylonia to kill a fellow Jew, or else be killed himself. The Jew hurried to a rabbi for guidance. The rabbi told the Jew that he had no right to kill the other man, but must accept death at the hand of the tyrant, even though he himself was innocent of any wrongdoing. Shedding the other Jew's blood, the rabbi said, was tantamount to planned murder and was, of course, strictly forbidden.

The famous biblical commentator Rashi taught that although Judaism allows a crime or a sin to be committed if it will save a life, this rule could not possibly be applied to murder, since this act would take, rather than save, a life. This principle applied even where the person who would be saved was a renowned scholar and the would-be murderer was a mere mortal. It may be, Rashi taught, that in God's eyes the scholar was not as saintly a person as the simple man.

During the Nazi Holocaust there were many cases of people trying to save loved ones at the expense of their own lives. There was even one young Hassid who told his Nazi captors that he was the leader of the Hassidic sect (he even donned the rabbi's clothes), believing that in doing so he could spare the life of a man who would be able to teach more Torah to more people than he himself could ever hope to do. The young Hassid was killed, and although he technically violated Jewish teaching, his motive could easily be seen as saintly and self-sacrificing, and thus forgivable.

And yet, despite its vigorous defense of life, Judaism simultaneously teaches: *Ha'kom l'horg'cha, hash'kem v'horgo*—he who comes to kill you, rise up early and kill him first. In this case the preemptive killer is preventing a premeditated murder, and this is wholly acceptable in Jewish law. However, to soften the harshness of the ruling the Talmud adds that, if it is possible for the intended victim to stave off the attacker by wounding him, he should do so. Killing him is a last resort.

* * *

Jews are often described as *rachmanim b'nai rachmanim*—compassionate sons of compassionate people. Nevertheless, in its teachings about justice and compassion, Judaism makes it clear that although justice should be tempered with mercy, it must not be swayed by emotional or non-legal factors. In other words, before the law, all men, rich and poor, kind and evil, are equal. The judge must determine the merits of a particular case and base his ruling solely on the facts set before him and on the laws that prevail.

Recognizing human foibles, the sages of old warned that "he who is compassionate to the cruel will in the end be cruel to the compassionate." Although Judaism regards compassion as one of the greatest of all human virtues, it does not totally eschew the negative emotion of hatred. "O, you who love the Lord," the psalmist wrote, "hate evil."

There is a poignant tale recorded in the Talmud about King David. He would sit in judgment in disputes and always acquit the innocent and punish the guilty; but if he saw that the condemned party was also a pauper, he would hand him some coins from his own purse. In this manner, the talmudic sages noted, he executed justice and doled out charity at the same time.

The etymology of the Hebrew word for justice, *tsedek*, is interesting. It is related to the Hebrew word *tsedaka*, meaning charity, for in Judaism charity is no more than a righting of a wrong, the substitution of justice for injustice. A person who is just and charitable is thus called a *tsadik*, usually translated as a righteous person. In Jewish life, to be described as a tsadik is the highest possible accolade.

On New York's Fifth Avenue, at the headquarters of the Reform Judaism movement in the United States, a memorable, significant quotation from the prophet Micah is engraved across the top of the building: "What does the Lord require of you: Only to do justly, and love mercy, and walk humbly with your God."

Justice for all is a paramount value of Judaism. The Bible exhorts us: "Justice, justice shall you pursue"; and, "Seek justice, relieve the oppressed. . . . Zion shall be redeemed with justice."

The Yiddish proverb puts it succinctly: "Rather suffer an injustice than commit one." The great British statesman, Benjamin Disraeli, who although he was baptized never ceased to boast of his Jewish background, declared in a speech to the House of Commons that "justice is truth in action."

The prophet Amos preached that God wanted no part of the Jews' worship if they were unjust: "Take away from Me the noise of your songs, and let Me not hear the melody of your psalteries—but let justice well up as waters, and righteousness as a mighty stream."

More than one historian has noted that there seems to be a disproportionately large number of Jews active in all movements to advance social justice in the world—as though they were still battling the ancient prophets' wars to bring about a totally just world for all peoples.

* * *

In Jewish tradition, man is "but a little lower than the angels"—and yet at the very same time Judaism teaches that we are like a mote of dust, fragile, transient, creatures that sustain ourselves and reproduce just like the lower animals. Thus, in Judaism's view, people are at one and the same time close to God and close to the animal kingdom. We are given freedom of choice, Jewish tradition says, but this freedom is limited. On the one hand, the Bible teaches that we are cast in the divine image, and certainly man's ability to think, to create, to perform good deeds, to make the world in which we live a better place—all these are virtually divine attributes.

Judaism however does not deceive itself. People are human—indeed, one cynical biblical phrase states: "The heart of man is bad from his earliest days." In the moving *Yizkor* memorial service, recited by loved ones in memory of those who have departed, the service opens with these poignant words:

"Lord, what is man that You pay attention to him? Or the son of man that You take account of him? Man is likened to vanity; his days are as a shadow that passes away. In the morning he flourishes and sprouts afresh, in the evening he is cut down and withers.

"Teach us to number our days so that we may get us a heart of wisdom. Mark the innocent man, and behold the upright, for the latter end of that man is peace. But God will redeem my soul from the grasp of the grave, for He will receive me. My flesh and my heart fail but God is the strength of my heart and my portion forever. And the dust returns to the earth as it was, but the spirit returns unto God who gave it. I shall behold Thy face in righteousness. I shall be satisfied, when I awake with Thy likeness."

A Jew is motivated and encouraged to move forward toward holiness throughout his or her life. Jews are aware of the fact that they possess earthly needs, that they must labor to earn their daily bread, that although there is much evil in the world there is also much good and beauty, and that they must always strive to bolster the beauty and sanctity around them. In so doing, they sense, they will add to their own spirituality, their own holiness.

Judaism places great emphasis on man's actions toward his fellow man. Thus, doing something sinful and then praying for forgiveness is not enough. The person against whom the evil deed was done must first reach out and forgive—then, and only then, will God extend forgiveness too.

＊　＊　＊

In Jewish tradition, there is a vast difference between wisdom and learning. A long time ago, in reference to people who study constantly and yet remain fools, a talmudic wit quipped that they were like "asses laden with books."

Nevertheless, Judaism regards learning and the pursuit of knowledge with reverence, with the conviction that in many cases learning will eventually lead to wisdom. Indeed, Judaism has incorporated study and learning into its very fabric. The highlight of the weekly Sabbath service are the cyclical Biblical and prophetic readings, which often elicit the rabbi's comments and reflections.

Sabbath afternoons, prior to the conclusion of the day of rest, are traditionally a time for group study in the synagogue—often comprising the Torah portion for the next week during the fall through spring months, and the less demanding *Ethics of the Fathers* (an anthology of biblical and talmudic axioms) in the summer months. Most synagogues, in addition, have regular adult education classes on subjects ranging from talmudic tractates to Jewish history or philosophy. Learning becomes second nature to a committed Jew; after a time, abstention from ongoing study makes him feel he is neglecting a vital religious commandment.

Jews are cautioned: "Set a time for study." The great Zionist philosopher Ahad Ha'am wrote in 1910: "Learning, learning, learning—that is the secret of Jewish survival." And millenia ago, Hillel taught: "He who does not learn forfeits his life." In the twelfth century, Maimonides wrote: "The advancement of learning is the highest commandment." The wise Yiddish writer, Mendele Mocher Sefarim, cautioned: "One may be learned and yet be a big fool." And Judah HaNassi taught: "I learned much from my teachers, more from my colleagues, and most from my pupils."

Despite its emphasis on study and learning, Judaism stresses that the goal of wisdom should always be held in the forefront of one's mind. And the Bible states: "The fear of the Lord, that is wisdom." The Bible also notes that although "wisdom is better than strength," at the same time "in much wisdom is much vexation."

The medieval poet and philosopher Moses ibn-Ezra said that "wisdom is like fire, a little enlightens—much burns." His contemporary, Avraham ibn-Ezra, wrote: "Wisdom begets humility"; while the biblical book of Proverbs stresses: "Happy is the man who finds wisdom. . . . Her ways are ways of pleasantness, and all her paths are peace. She is a tree of life to those who lay hold of her."

Judaism emphasizes that wisdom begins with the acceptance of God's rule. Thus, life is to be made up of holiness, good deeds, learning, the attainment of wisdom, and with it serenity, fulfillment and wholeness.

One issue that does not confront Jews is the struggle between the flesh and the spirit. In Jewish tradition, both the body and the spirit are hallowed and should be filled with suitable sustenance. Of course, Judaism is opposed to extremism, be it ascetic or Epicurean. The desires of the flesh are not held to be evil, but it is believed that they should be channeled and controlled. Sensuality that is uninhibited is condemned by Judaism, as is self-denial of the natural desires of the body. From a religious standpoint, Judaism states, man is obliged to enjoy life, physically, spiritually, emotionally, in every suitable manner.

Judaism looks upon the sexual impulse with a wise eye. In the words of Rabbi Nachman ben Shmuel it says: "If not for the 'evil impulse,'—i.e., the sexual impulse—no man would ever build a house, take a wife, beget a child, or engage in business."

CHAPTER EIGHT
UNDERSTANDING GOD—WITHOUT DOGMA

IN THE EARLY 1920S THERE LIVED IN FRANCE A YOUNG French Jewish dramatist by the name of Edmond Fleg. Although he came from an outwardly observant Jewish home, he was himself a non-practicing Jew. The Jewish community at the time was deeply assimilationist, and Judaism *per se* meant little to most French Jews. This situation changed radically after World War II, when French Jews had learned to their horror that many of their compatriots were ready to denounce them to the Nazi occupiers. The establishment of Israel in 1948, the aftermath of the Holocaust, and the arrival of large numbers of traditional Jews from former French colonies in North Africa changed the French Jewish community almost overnight. It is now the fourth largest in the world, after the United States, Israel and the Soviet Union, and has become very dynamic, activist and committed.

Back in the 1920s, many French Jews, including Fleg,

believed that the road to success in life lay in crossing over to the majority Catholic community. He considered seriously doing so, but decided that before making the break he would do some reading about Judaism. This exercise swiftly changed his mind. Judaism, he learned, was a deeply precious heritage, a way of life that afforded spiritual and ethical sustenance. In a memorable small book, *Why I Am A Jew,* he wrote to his unborn grandson: "I am a Jew because in all places where there are tears and suffering, the Jew weeps . . . because in every age when the cry of despair is heard, the Jew hopes . . . because for the Jewish people the world is not completed— men will complete it."

Fleg also said: "I am a Jew because the faith of Judaism demands no abdication of my mind . . . because the message of Israel is the most ancient and simultaneously the most modern . . . because Israel's promise is a universal promise."

* * *

One of the most ongoing and difficult controversies within the Jewish community, at least among theologians, rabbis and scholars, has been the question: Does Judaism have a set of dogmas that can be put down on paper and pointed to as the essential beliefs of the Jewish religion? Some authorities answer with a resounding no, while others, equally passionate, respond in the affirmative.

Those who insist that Judaism is without dogma challenge their opponents to cite prescriptive statements, from the Bible, Talmud, or any other ancient or recent Jewish text. The ancient religious legislative body of the Jewish people, the *Sanhedrin,* which was in existence for some seven hundred years, never issued a blueprint for what Judaism is, or what is required of a Jew.

Efforts at formulating a basic statement of principles, including Maimonides' famous "Thirteen Principles of Faith," were never universally accepted. Through the centuries, one or more of those principles has always been under debate by Jewish theologians, and they are generally placed in the back of a prayerbook and not actually incorporated into the service.

Another compelling reason for the lack of a hard and fast formula describing Judaism is that through the centuries, Jews have not really come to an agreement on all aspects of Judaism's teachings. One need but look at the Talmud, that incredibly daunting set of volumes that consists of commentaries, rulings, discussions, interpretations and laws based on the Bible. In almost all cases, the decisions of the majority are given alongside the thoughts of the minority. Indeed, an objective critic looking at the Talmud would immediately discern that this is a strange mixture of contributions from rationalists, mystics, literalists, allegorists, liberal interpreters, rigid commentators—a real hodgepodge of centuries of creative thinking. And yet, strangely, it hangs together. Jews have very individual approaches to explaining their concept of God. Even in some Orthodox congregations there are observant members who simply follow the rules, trusting that in the course of time they will mature enough and learn enough to understand what is meant by the word *God*. Reform and Conservative Jews, including those who are active, committed, hard-working, may confess that they lean more toward the Torah learning and Jewish peoplehood aspects of Judaism than to the idea of faith in God, but in most cases they will keep an open mind in the expectation that as they grow older they will understand better the meaning of the term *God*.

The conception of God is also affected by an often-unexpressed but nevertheless powerful Holocaust factor. Many Jews are, as it were, mad at God. They cannot understand why God permitted the Holocaust to occur, and the explanations sometimes offered, that God turned His face away, or that it was all part of a master plan which is unfathomable to us, do not wash. Rather than deny the existence of God, these Jews recite prayers, bless God for His bounty, thank Him for all the wonders of life, and yet harbor deep in their hearts a gnawing, unceasing question: Why? Why God, did You let it happen?

On the other side of the issue of dogma, there is of course a school of thought which insists that Judaism, like most other faiths, does have a set of fundamental values, and that these convictions have shaped the Jewish people through its long existence. Over the centuries, Judaism has fought against idolatry, battled what it considered the specious, false values of Greek and Roman culture, and still later fought off the encroachments of a powerful Christian church, especially from the onset of the Middle Ages. Nowadays, Judaism must continue to do battle, with atheism, crass materialism, cults of various kinds, aggressive missionary groups, post-Hiroshima nihilism. Without some set of basic principles, this pro-dogma school of thought contends, Judaism could not wage these battles.

There is at present no easy, hard and fast way to decide which of the two schools of thought is correct. Both have some merit. That is, Judaism certainly has strongly-held religious principles, but it is reluctant to turn them into hard laws that must be obeyed. Why? Probably because unlike the Ten Commandments, whose rationale is evident to all, a set of dogmas spelling out Jewish belief would not apply to large numbers of people for the simple reason that Jews in different stages of their lives hold changing views of God, Judaism, faith. In other words, instead of declaring that to be a Jew one must recite this code and abide by it, the feeling is that it is far better to perform acts of kindness, to enjoy a day of Sabbath rest, to learn the wisdom of the Torah, to be moved by a religious service, to be inspired by a rabbi's sermon—these acts of living as a Jew are seen as more effective than memorizing a dogma at a tender age, perhaps not fully understanding it, and repeating it without full appreciation until one's later years. In effect, Judaism teaches: do, practice, perform, and faith and belief will follow. It is really an echo of the old Jewish teaching—deeds count, not words.

There is yet another reason why Judaism has been chary of setting down a formal, dogmatic code. The followers of Judaism are not only members of a religious congregation, but they are also part of a nationality, or if you will, a nation. And as residents of whatever country they live in, they owe their allegiance to that country—a set of dogmatic, religious principles might set them off even more from the rest of the country. In every country in which they live (except Israel) Jews are a minority, and guarding their rights is always at the top of their communal agenda. There is a feeling that spelling out a creed or a code of principles might alienate them even more from the mainstream majority.

Of course there is still another major reason why Judaism does not have a formal set of rules—it is, as has been noted, a very historic, very ancient faith, and over the centuries there have been, and continue to be, a wide gamut of interpreters, each of who brings a unique insight to Judaism and Jewish practice. It is feared that a set dogma would still these voices, and Judaism must continue to be a religion in which everyone—rabbi and layman alike—has an equal right to express a view, form an opinion, and offer an explanation. Although Judaism is far from being a do-it-yourself faith, for there most certainly are established rules, regulations, traditions and customs, it is nevertheless relatively libertarian, in that each Jew may comment and interpret to the best of his ability.

A wise rabbi teaching a class of adults, for example, might choose a biblical passage, read it aloud, and then ask his students to comment. Chances are that he will receive highly individual interpretations, based on the students' own backgrounds, knowledge of Judaism, or intuition—and in a very meaningful way, all of these variegated explications will be valid. A formal, official creed is feared in Judaism as a potential restraint on free thought.

Furthermore, in Jewish belief, reason and logic and the intellect—although highly valued—do not compare with morality, mercy, and justice. Ethical life is first and foremost the noble ideal to strive for, and it is felt that this in turn will lead to a personal, religious credo.

* * *

One of the most unappreciated books of Jewish wisdom is a small work, usually called in English, *Ethics of the Fathers*. This is an anthology of pithy sayings, axioms and words of counsel taken from various biblical and talmudic sources, whose principal motivation is to teach people to be better, kinder, wiser, more compassionate and caring, more benevolent, more selfless—in the greater sense of the term, more *religious*.

There will always be people who will question this whole concept: Can goodness be taught? Can a person who is essentially selfish and egocentric learn to become kind and giving? Judaism seems to think the answer is positive; at the very least, it seems to say, we have to try.

Some of Judaism's basic teachings and beliefs are to be found in *Ethics of the Fathers*. For example:

"Upon three things does the world rest—on the Torah, on worship of God, and on the performance of acts of loving-kindness."

"Let your house be a place of assembly for the wise, sit amidst the dust of their feet, and drink in their words with thirst."

"Let your house be wide open, let the poor be members of your household. Do not engage in gossip with women; this applies to one's own wife, so all the more so with a neighbor's wife."

"Get yourself a teacher, find yourself a friend, and judge all people charitably."

"Do not associate with the wicked, stay far away from a bad neighbor, and do not give up the concept of retribution."

"Be like the students of Aaron—love peace, pursue peace,

love your fellow creatures, and draw them closer to the Torah."

"If I am not for myself, who will be? But if I am only for myself, what am I? And if not now, when?"

"Set a time for the study of Torah; say little and do much; receive all people with a cheerful face."

"An empty-headed man cannot be sin-fearing, nor can an ignorant person be truly pious."

"Do not separate yourself from the community. Do not judge your fellow man until you are in his place. Do not say anything that cannot be understood immediately. Do not say, 'When I have time I will study.' Perhaps you will have no time."

"The more flesh, the more worms. The more property, the more anxiety. The more wives, the more witchcraft. The more maid servants, the more lewdness. The more men servants, the more robbery. But—the more Torah, the more life. The more schooling, the more wisdom. The more counsel, the more understanding. The more charity, the more peace."

"It is not your duty to complete a task, but neither are you free to avoid it."

"Know from whence you came, where you are going, and to Whom you will have to give account in the future."

"Pray for the welfare of the government, since but for the fear of it men would swallow each other alive."

"He whose deeds exceed his wisdom, his wisdom will endure. But he whose wisdom exceeds his deeds, his wisdom will not endure."

* * *

Judaism, like other religions, encourages people to be considerate of one another and to demonstrate concern for a fellow human being through concrete acts of charity. However, even when being charitable, a person must respect the recipient of his largess, and display respect, discretion and understanding. Indeed, Maimonides taught that there are eight degrees of charity, and this enumerated list has become a well-established component of Jewish life. Of the eight degrees, the last is the highest.

The first degree is exemplified by a person who gives charity, but does so with regret, or grudgingly. Second degree: a person who gives graciously but donates less than the maximum which he can afford. Third: a person who gives the full amount, but does so only after he has been solicited. Fourth: someone who gives even before he is asked. Fifth: a person who gives without knowing who the recipient is, although the latter knows the identity of the donor. Sixth: an anonymous donor. Seventh: someone who gives charity without knowing who the recipient is, and without the recipient knowing who the donor is. Eighth: a person who helps someone in need, through a gift or loan or by finding them employment, to become self-supporting, and thus to leave the roster of the needy.

* * *

Non-Jews may well mistakenly believe that Judaism encroaches on a person's privacy. After all, there are religious laws and rules about getting up in the morning, about morning prayers, washing the hands before meals, reciting blessings before the meal and saying grace afterwards, attending services morning and evening, taking time out to study; on Sabbaths and holidays the rules are changed, with special strictures on dress for the synagogue, eating festive meals and accompanying them with suitable singing. On the Sabbath's approach (Friday evening) there is the *kiddush* (wine sanctification) ceremony, and when the Sabbath ends with sundown on Saturday, there is a *havdalah* (separation) ceremony. Holidays are marked by distinctive observances—special foods for Passover, candle-lighting ceremonies for Hanukkah, the public reading of the Book of Esther on Purim, dancing with the Torahs on Simhat Torah, dining in a *sukkah* (a hut) on Sukkot,

special services on Rosh Hashanah, fasting on Yom Kippur—
and there are still other occasions to be celebrated, enjoyed,
commemorated. A person who loses a parent, for example, is
required to recite the daily *kaddish* prayer for nearly a year—on
the anniversary of his or her death *(yahrzeit)* and at special
yizkor (memorial) services held on Passover, Shavuot, Yom
Kippur, and Shmini Atzeret. It is customary to light a memorial candle on the decedent's yahrzeit and on Yom Kippur.

It is understandable that people sometimes ask, when do
you have time to relax, time to unwind, to do what you enjoy
doing?

The question is understandable, and to someone not
brought up in a traditional Jewish home it may seem that a
whole lot of time is given over to prayers and services and for
not much else. This is of course silly. Jews who are observant
and follow all or most of the traditions and regulations find
time for everything. In Judaism time is a very special phenomenon; it is constantly being assessed. There is an appointed
time for kindling the Sabbath lights on Friday; there is an
appointed time when the Sabbath begins and the mundane
daily world is left behind, when a family snatches a day of
delight and rest and relaxation from the rest of the week—if
properly celebrated, Sabbath becomes a day of physical, psychological, spiritual rest, a day given over to prayer, study,
song and joy. A traditional Jewish family offers up on the
Sabbath a picture of true serenity that is rare in our fast-paced
world, and quite beautiful.

* * *

Judaism has been transposed over the centuries from monotheistic religion with a priestly class and a Holy Temple, in
which animal sacrifices were offered in supplication and
thanks to the Almighty, into a religious way of life that stresses
ethical living, deeds of kindness, compassion for all human
beings, a strong commitment to the welfare of the Jewish

people, a firm but often ineffable belief in God with whom the Jewish people has an eternal covenant, and a powerful commitment to a lifelong study and understanding of the Torah.

Professor Louis Ginzburg, who was one of the outstanding teachers at the Jewish Theological Seminary of America, taught that the Jewish nation "survived the downfall of its state and the destruction of its national sanctuary" because of the "genius of Rabbi Johanan ben Zakai, who made of religious study a new form in which the national existence of the Jews found expression—so that side by side with the history of nearly two thousand years of suffering we can point to an equally extensive history of intellectual effort. Studying and wandering, thinking and enduring, learning and suffering, fill this long period.

"Thinking is as characteristic a trait of the Jew as suffering, or to be more exact, thinking rendered suffering possible. For it was our thinkers who prevented the wandering nation, this true 'wandering Jew' from sinking to the level of brutalized vagrants, of vagabond gypsies."

In Judaism performing a *mitzvah*—a religious commandment—has a double meaning—it is both a commandment, and a source of gratification. A truly traditional Jew, therefore, does not look upon his religious duties as a burdensome duty but rather as a religious duty that will also afford him joy. A Jewish man, for example, who wraps himself in a prayer shawl *(tallit)* and puts on his phylacteries *(tefilin* in Hebrew)—little leather boxes containing scriptural passages, worn on the head and on the arm—at the start of his weekday morning services, recites this beautiful verse from the prophet Hosea: "I will betroth you unto Me forever. Yes, I will betroth you unto Me in righteousness, and in justice, and in loving kindness, and in compassion. And I will betroth you unto Me in faithfulness, and you shall know the Lord."

In other words, every weekday morning (tefilin are not used on the Sabbath), a worshiper dons the little black boxes, wraps himself in a *tallit* (prayer shawl), and repeats God's promise to the Jewish people as enunciated by Hosea, that God and the Jewish people are betrothed to one another, in righteousness, loving kindness, justice, compassion, and faithfulness.

Could there really be a better way to start the day's activities?

CHAPTER NINE
SABBATH AND HOLIDAYS

TO A GENTILE, THE STRESS THAT JUDAISM PLACES ON FULL observance of the Sabbath and the Jewish holidays and festivals may seem excessive. Why, one may wonder, should one of the Ten Commandments—ten per cent—be devoted exclusively to ruling that the Sabbath day should be "remembered" and kept holy? Is the concept of a day's rest from a week's hard work such an important, religious institution? Doesn't everyone who works hard look forward to a relaxing and restful weekend, and to vacations and holidays?

Judaism evolved in a time when most people worked very hard, and probably looked upon taking time off from labor as wasteful. In an agricultural society in particular there is always something to do—a farmer or a vintner or a shepherd could easily work from dawn till sundown, seven days a week, and not realize that his humanity was draining away from him and that he was turning into a drudge.

The Sabbath developed not only as a required day of rest, but as a day of spiritual refreshment. To put it another way, every seventh day—the Sabbath day—was designed to emphasize the Jew's humanity, to link him closer with God, to make him understand that a man must achieve in his daily life a sense of serenity and peace, a feeling of inner restfulness that is far beyond the mere cessation of physical labor.

That is why the Sabbath has over the centuries been transformed into a weekly celebration of God, a taste, as some would have it, of the world to come. Properly observed, the Sabbath becomes a day of relaxation from mundane daily chores, a day to concentrate on study, song and contemplation, to dress for a festive occasion, to take time to walk and talk with children, with one's spouse, with friends and relatives, to shut out the intrusive world for twenty-four hours and shut in a world of spirituality and inner happiness.

The Bible states that God calls the Sabbath day a "sign between Me and the children of Israel forever." The Sabbath has been referred to as the "heart of Judaism," and the heroic rabbi Leo Baeck, who survived a Nazi concentration camp, described it as meant "to give man peaceful hours, hours completely diverted from everyday life, seclusion from the world in the midst of the world."

The British author Israel Zangwill sums it up beautifully: "Sabbath is the hub of the Jew's universe—to protect it is a virtue, to live it is a liberal education." Rabbi Mordecai Kaplan, the founder of the Reconstructionist movement in American Judaism, taught that an "artist cannot be continually wielding his brush. He must stop at times in his painting to freshen his vision of the object, the meaning of which he wishes to express on his canvas. Living is also an art . . . and the Sabbath represents those moments when we pause in our brushwork to renew our vision of the object."

Orthodox, Conservative, Reform and Reconstructionist Jews observe the Sabbath differently, at least outwardly. Those Jews who do observe, to one degree or another, share part of the substance of the Sabbath day. Among the Orthodox Jewish community, the rules for keeping the Sabbath are precise and rigid, and generally speaking members of this community adhere to the rules fully.

Halachah (Jewish religious law) guides the Orthodox and Conservative movements but is largely eschewed by the Reform and Reconstructionist groupings. But even among the Orthodox there are variations and gradations of observance, and among the Conservative there are rather liberal interpretations which some Orthodox Jews regard as bordering on heresy. For example, driving a car on the Sabbath day of rest is taboo in Jewish religious law. Most Orthodox Jews reside within a short walking distance of their synagogues, most of which are small in size. The Conservative Jews, on the other hand, tend to favor larger buildings, which are often located a few miles from members' homes, usually in the suburbs. How can a Conservative Jew attend synagogue on the Sabbath if it is too far to walk?

Pragmatically, the Conservative rabbis some years ago met and agreed that driving to the synagogue on the Sabbath or a Jewish holy day is permissible—it is better to drive to synagogue than to stay home and not participate in congregational services. No other driving, however, is permitted.

To a traditional, Orthodox Jew this is unacceptable. The moment a person inserts a key into the car's ignition and starts the car, he has lost the magical spirit that up to that point elevated the day of Sabbath rest; for him, driving to synagogue is an oxymoron. He will contend further that Conservative Jews, once they become accustomed to driving to services, will then not feel so badly about driving to see a friend in the afternoon, or to a golf course, or whatever.

Many Conservative rabbis would probably agree, and many of them do walk to services, however far away, so as to enjoy the full spirit of the Sabbath, and not let it be interrupted by the firing of an automobile engine.

Whether a family is strictly Orthodox, moderately Conservative, or wholly Reform, the Sabbath day is meant to be observed in a set, definite manner. Families observe the rituals

and precepts in a wide array of styles; some make compro-
mises because of economic necessity (many men have to work
on Saturdays), some make adjustments because their busy
schedules only allow an attenuated form of observance, and
others genuinely believe that they are observing and hallowing
the Sabbath day in their own, perhaps somewhat esoteric,
manner.

The Sabbath begins on sundown on Friday, and ends on
sundown on Saturday. Just before the sun sets on Friday,
Sabbath candles are kindled in the home, generally by the
wife/mother, often surrounded by her family. She lights the
candles, covers her eyes, recites an appropriate blessing, and
everyone wishes one another *Shabbat Shalom*—a peaceful Sabbath. The husband/father will (in an Orthodox household) go
to the synagogue for Sabbath eve services, and on his return
the family will sit down together for a festive meal, at which
religious songs—known as *z'mirot*—are often sung between
courses. In a Conservative or Reform family, Sabbath eve
dinner will usually follow the kindling of the candles, after
which the family will attend late Friday services, usually beginning at 8:30 P.M. This service usually lasts an hour or less, and
is generally followed by an *Oneg Shabbat,* a Sabbath social, at
which the congregants will sit together, drink tea and coffee,
eat light refreshments, and sometimes hear a talk by the rabbi
or a guest speaker. This congregational-communal sense of
Sabbath, of belonging, are often warm moments in the participants' lives. Many of the men who attend Friday night services
and the Oneg Shabbat will be absent from Saturday morning
services, either because they have to work, or because—among
some Reform and Conservative Jews—there is a feeling that
one service a week is ample, and Saturdays they may go off to
a golf course, a tennis court, or a beach

This is not the prescribed, traditional Jewish way of celebrating and hallowing the Sabbath, but this is how things
evolve and who knows?—there may very well be a rabbi in the
not too distant future who will argue that the essential object

of the Sabbath day is rest, and if some people find it more restful lobbing a tennis ball than listening to a cantor or a rabbi's sermon, then that is all to the good.

The Sabbath itself is meant to be a day of prayer, study, song, contemplation, spirituality. At Sabbath morning services the congregation joins in songs that are only sung on the Sabbath. The Torah reading that is read and studied is designed to give the congregants an opportunity to understand a fresh biblical insight, and to relate it, if possible, to an issue of the day.

At the end of the morning Saturday service, which can last between two and a half to three and a half hours, there is usually a *kiddush,* a reception where congregants munch on some tidbits, sip some drinks (both soft and alcoholic), socialize, talk with friends, review the rabbi's sermon (out of his earshot, of course), congratulate the day's celebrants (a bar or bat mitzvah youth, an *ofruf* (a groom about to be married), or parents of a new-born girl who has just been named in the synagogue). People are dressed up, the mood is festive, the atmosphere relaxing, and people spend a quarter-hour or so discussing events of the day, local news, congregational activities, and personal happenings.

A stranger attending such a kiddush might be excused if he assumes that this is a big family gathering, since there is so much animated talk, cheek-kissing, laughter, and warmth. Although it is not really a family, in the best sense it often is seen as an extended family. When a congregant sustains a personal loss, the consolation extended by the other members is often a very deep source of comfort and support.

After Sabbath services, families generally sit down to a festive meal at home. As on Friday night, there is a special blessing for wine, known as *kiddush;* and a special blessing over the white Sabbath bread *(chalah),* usually known as *ha'motsee.* After the meal, people will often spend the afternoon napping, visiting, reading, or walking. Among some Conservative, and probably most Reform, Jews who are celebrating the Sabbath, music may be heard in the house, on radio or tape or phonograph.

Towards evening, congregants will return to the synagogue for the closing service of the day—a combination afternoon *(mincha)* and evening *(ma'ariv)* service, which on Saturday late-afternoon/evening also features the reading of a small part of next week's Torah portion, as well as the beautiful *havdalah* (separation) service. Here, the person leading the service lights a special candle, blesses a goblet of wine, for a moment inhales some incense, and with a traditional melody sings away the Sabbath, separating it, as it were, from the mundane, week's work. The Sabbath Queen departs, people feel, as they prepare to resume their weekday schedules, confident that she will be back on Friday evening, bringing in her wake joy and rest. As they leave the synagogue, congregants call out to one another, in Yiddish, *Gute Voch,* or in Hebrew, *Shavua Tov*—Have a good week!

Is it any wonder that the Zionist essayist and philosopher Ahad Ha'am said that "more than Israel kept the Sabbath, the Sabbath has kept Israel." Rabbi Baeck taught that "there is no Judaism without the Sabbath." Among certain Hassidic sects there is a mystical belief that if only all Jews in every part of the world would observe the Sabbath fully and totally, in all its minutiae, then the Messiah will arrive and usher in the messianic age.

In an essay written in 1923, Rabbi Benno Jacob said: "The Sabbath is the greatest wonder of religion. Nothing can appear more simple than this institution. Yet no legislator hit upon this idea! To the Greeks and Romans it was an object of derision, a superstitious usage. But it removed with one stroke a contrast between slaves who must labor incessantly and their masters who may celebrate continuously." Or as Claude Montefiore wrote in 1903: "The Sabbath prevents us reducing our lives to the level of a machine. If to labor is noble, of our own free will to pause in that labor may be nobler still."

There can be little doubt that the Sabbath is a central component of Judaism, and a major source of strength for observant, practicing Jews. The recent phenomenon—which is now virtually worldwide—of young men proudly announcing their return to traditional Judaism by wearing small yarmulkes at work in schools, courtrooms, hospitals and elsewhere has been advanced in recent years because of the enjoyment that these *Baalei-T'shuva* (penitents) experienced when they immersed themselves in a traditional Sabbath atmosphere.

For many young Jews reared in traditional homes, the Sabbath probably sometimes appeared to be repressive. "Everyone" was off to a ball game or the seashore or whatever, and they were persuaded to stay home and celebrate the Jewish day of rest peacefully, with parents and siblings. Many of these young people, both those from traditional and only marginally observant homes, broke away from religious observance as soon as they were old enough to move away from their parents' home, and set up for themselves.

Most of these people married and had children, and then a funny thing happened as their own children grew, and as they matured—slowly in some cases, instantly in others, many of these same people, now that they were adults themselves, began to fathom that the Sabbath, and indeed all of Judaism, was something to be cherished, observed and enjoyed. And thus began the spin of a new cycle, as the young parents accompanied their own children to religious school and/or to synagogue, they too began in many cases to appreciate that one day off from the swift, tense week was a glorious idea, and they started to observe the Sabbath pretty much the same way their own parents had wanted them to do.

Sabbath, wrote Rabbi Abraham Joshua Heschel, one of the greatest Jewish thinkers of the twentieth century, is nothing less than a "gift." It is a day when "we celebrate creation, we sanctify Shabbat with all our senses. Struggle and dissonance are forgotten, we are surrounded by peace and wholeness. Shabbat is a temple in time . . . it is holiness in time, the presence of eternity, a moment of majesty . . . Sabbath ennobles, enhances; it nourishes the seed of eternity planted in our soul. Shabbat is a gift of dignity and of rest, of holiness, splendor and delight . . . a time of peace, tranquility, harmony and joy."

* * *

Jews consider Judaism a faith of reason. There is a need sometimes for a "leap of faith" in order to begin the process of understanding, but once one is committed to living a Jewish life, and approaches all religious problems logically, asking questions, seeking responses, one realizes that although not all answers can satisfy fully at all times, there is nonetheless a rational, intellectual basis for faith.

At some point, many people reach an understanding of the life around them in which they come to realize that life without some form of religious belief is unsatisfying. This realization sometimes arrives with a shock, as when a soldier is in grave peril on the battlefield and he reaches out to a Power greater than himself for help. It may come as a young mother gives birth to a healthy baby, and it dawns on her that this miracle of a baby born of her own flesh and blood must somehow have some link to a Higher Power.

Judaism *per se* is more a whole way of life than it is a religious faith; it is concerned with every aspect of life, twenty-four hours a day and seven days a week. Judaism recommends certain laws, rules and customs that it believes will bring inner happiness and fulfillment as a human being—in this world. There is not one word in the Torah about heaven or hell, nor is there any promise that good deeds will be rewarded or bad deeds will be punished in the next world. These are foreign concepts, which have crept into Judaism, too, but they are not part of Judaism's basic tenets. Judaism seems to say: "God says obey these rules, do good deeds, and don't worry about what happens after you die. Life will be rewarding here on earth, if you do the right thing." In other's words, God's kingdom is right here, on earth.

*   *   *

One of the major ways in which a Jew lives his Judaism is through celebrating the Jewish holidays and festivals. Of course, if he is an American, he celebrates America's holidays too, so that his year-round calendar is a crowded document. Thus, as an American a Jew will celebrate the Fourth of July, Labor Day, Thanksgiving Day, Memorial Day; if he is a veteran, he may march with other veterans on July fourth and/or on Memorial Day. Chances are that Thanksgiving Day will be a big family get-together—nowadays, many Jewish families find that their offspring are scattered to the proverbial four corners and parents are delighted if they can see their grown children (and of course grandchildren) at least three or four times a year. A new kind of pattern has developed in recent years—families get together not only for the Passover seder which usually falls in late March or April, but also during the High Holy Days (September or October) and late November (Thanksgiving Day). They also get together in many cases during the Hanukkah-Christmas-New Year's vacation period toward the end of the year, and sometimes in February during the presidential birthday periods. Of course, efforts are also made for visits during the summer vacation months, but this is also a time when many people are either traveling or their children are away at camp.

At any rate, in addition to all the secular holidays, and those special occasions when families try to get together, traditional Jewish families also celebrate the Jewish year's events, beginning with the High Holy Days, a ten-day period that usually falls in September and begins with *Rosh Hashanah* (New Year) and ends on *Yom Kippur* (Day of Atonement). Large parts of the day of Rosh Hashanah are spent at prayer services; on Yom Kippur practically the entire day is spent in prayer and fasting.

This ten-day period represents an annual spiritual renewal. A Jew looks back on the year just past, and thinks of the year about to begin. He recites the ancient words, phrases such as: "We have sinned, we have transgressed, by the act of commission, and by the act of omission." A worshiper must probe his innermost self, honestly and courageously: If he did something of which he says he is now ashamed, is he truly remorseful? Is he now really ready to turn over a new leaf and become a more righteous person? This is the spirit that permeates the Jewish community during this ten-day period of the High Holy Days.

Actually, most people during this period tend to have a hopeful attitude toward the new year and the kind of life that they and their loved ones will have. In other words, most people feel that they have lived good, decent lives; however, as they read the prayers, in which various sinful acts are described in detail, some people may hesitate and wonder about themselves and their own morality.

The confessional parts of the High Holy Day services are poignant and moving, but there are no individual confessions. All the prayers, all the sins, all the evil deeds, the prayerbook states, were committed by "us"—by the entire congregation, by the entire community. Thus, if Mr. A. is standing and praying alongside Mr. B., and A. knows that he is a good and decent man, and he is also convinced that his neighbor is a terrible sinner, he finds that both of them are nonetheless reciting the same communal confession—"We have sinned, we have transgressed, we have done such and such." A. will soon realize that even if he himself is innocent, it behooves him to try to bring B. back to the straight and narrow. In other words, the entire people must be turned toward paths of holiness, justice, goodness.

The eve of the High Holy Days is informed by the strong

Jewish tradition that God does not forgive anyone who has sinned against a person if that person has not yet forgiven the sinner. It is therefore not so unusual for traditional Jews to greet each other with best wishes for the New Year before the holiday, and then to add, "If I offended or insulted you during the year, please forgive me. I'm sorry."

It is customary on Rosh Hashanah to enjoy a piece of chalah bread dipped in honey, to symbolize the sweet new year that is hoped will be inscribed for that particular individual. There is a belief that on Rosh Hashanah God inscribes every person's fate for the coming year, and makes up His mind during the ten-day High Holy Days period whether that will indeed become that person's fate. At the close of Yom Kippur, so the tradition goes, God seals one's fate for good. That is why, early in the High Holy Days period, people wish each other a *k'teeva tovah*—a good inscription, and then on Yom Kippur, *chateema tovah*—a good sealing-in.

Although many people devote considerable time and expense to dressing up for Rosh Hashanah and Yom Kippur, and to the holiday meals, they remain very spiritual holidays. Even the most jaded people cannot but be deeply affected when the cantor chants the words of the prayer which acknowledge that we do not know "who will live, and who will die, who in his proper time, and who not in his proper time" in the coming year. Few worshipers remain unmoved when the cantor, or the rabbi, or some other synagogue official recalls the names of those congregants who died in the previous year.

Rosh Hashanah and Yom Kippur together form a unique, introspective holiday in which worshipers feel extraordinarily close to God and to their religious heritage.

Immediately after the High Holy Days, Sukkot and Simhat Torah are celebrated in another long holiday period, of nine days (eight for Reform Jews), which recalls the time when the Israelites, fleeing from the Egyptians, lived in the wilderness in temporary homes, in booths or *sukkot* in Hebrew (the holiday is called more fancifully, Tabernacles). Sukkot is also the harvest holiday in Israel, when the last of the year's produce is brought in. One of the special features of this holiday—in addition to the custom of eating in little booths erected near the family home—is the use of the *lulav* and *etrog*—the former is a palm frond which is bound together with a small branch from a myrtle and another from a willow; the latter is a citron, a fruit of the citrus family.

The use of these agricultural products during Sukkot is of course related to the harvest aspect of this holiday, but their symbolism is very spiritual. The citron, which is usually larger than a lemon and resembles it in form somewhat, is a fruit that is both aromatic and has a good taste—representing a person who is steeped in learning and who also performs good deeds.

The palm frond reminds us that the tree bears fruit but has no pleasant aroma—therefore, it represents people who are rich in money but poor in good deeds.

The myrtle (*hadas* in Hebrew) has a pleasant aroma but no taste—it represents people who possess learning but do not use their knowledge for society's benefit.

And the willow (*aravah* in Hebrew) has no pleasant aroma and is not edible, and therefore stands for a person who lacks learning, lacks money, and is also without good deeds.

During the Sukkot services it is almost awesome to watch as the male congregants, clad in prayer shawls and holding the etrog in the left hand, and the lulav combined with the other branches in the right, march around the synagogue, chanting centuries-old liturgical verses, and representing the oneness of all people, good, bad, rich, poor, learned, uneducated, in the overall scheme of life. The cantor also leads the congregation in asking God for His blessings on the land and its yield.

The little booths in which Jews eat at least some of their meals during the Sukkot festival are meant to represent the makeshift homes that the ancient Israelites occupied when they lived in the wilderness, as they fled Egypt for the Promised Land.

They also symbolize the fragility of life and the superficiality of material possessions. Thus, even if a Jewish family lives in a solid, comfortable home, Judaism teaches that it is good for them to remember what is really important in life. Riches, possessions, material goods—these are all fleeting; only a life committed to goodness, justice and compassion is meaningful.

The eighth day of the Sukkot holiday is known as *Shmini Atzeret,* and it is a day when congregants pray for ample rains in Israel—an ancient problem and one that still confronts Israel to this day. In Israel and among Reform Jews, this holiday and the one that follows on the next day—Simhat Torah—are celebrated on the same day.

Simhat Torah—literally, the joy of Torah—marks the completion of the year-long reading of weekly portions of the Torah, and the start of a new cycle in the new year that began a few weeks earlier, on Rosh Hashanah. In most synagogues this is an occasion for merrymaking and unfettered joy; sometimes rabbis, cantors and laymen will attend the service on this holiday in costume, or clown hats, or sport false beards—anything to lend a festive, fun atmosphere to the proceedings.

The main event of the holiday is the procession of the Scrolls of the Law around the synagogue; everybody is expected to carry a scroll or at least stand around, singing, chanting, and kissing the Torah as it passes by. Seven *hakafot,* or circuits, are usually made of the synagogue as the Torahs are borne around the sanctuary. Then, ceremoniously, the last portion of Deuteronomy is read aloud and almost at once the opening passage of Genesis is begun, and the new cyclical reading of the Torah is launched.

It is also customary for very small children, too young to understand what is going on, to be given small flags to carry, sometimes crowned by apples. Those youngsters who do understand but who are too young to carry a Torah are generally called up together to the Torah, where a very large prayer shawl is extended to cover them all as a collective blessing is recited for them.

For people who have never visited a synagogue, it might be useful at this point to describe a Jewish house of worship. Like most churches, the synagogue features a sanctuary where worship services are held and which of course is the holiest area of the building. Most synagogues also have classrooms for religious studies, a library, a hall for catered receptions and an office.

Conservative and Reform synagogues in recent years have begun to add stained glass windows, whose motifs are biblical narratives. In the synagogue proper, there are regular seats, which may be individual (as in a theater) or group seats. Some synagogue seats are emblazoned with a family's name, indicating a sizable contribution to the congregation.

The front of the sanctuary features a raised platform, called a *beemah,* where the rabbi, the cantor and one or more officers of the congregation are seated. A table on the beemah holds the Torah scroll when it is read aloud. The back of the beemah is where the scrolls are kept when not in use, in an ark called the Holy Ark, above which hangs a permanently-lit light called the Eternal Light.

During the service, congregants are usually seated, except when the Torah is carried about or when it is raised on high, when everyone rises as a sign of respect. The congregation also recites certain prayers while standing—the silent *amidah* prayer, the mourners' *kaddish, alainoo,* and a few others. There is no kneeling in a synagogue except, oddly, at certain points in the High Holy Days service, the rabbi and the cantor both prostrate themselves briefly in front of the Holy Ark. Congregants designated to help them rise consider it an honor to do so.

There is no collection plate in the synagogue, but during weekday services there is a "pushka," an alms box for the poor and needy. A synagogue may also be called a temple, and especially among traditional Jews it is often referred to as a "shul."

The next major holiday in the Jewish calendar is *Hanukkah,* a very popular celebration in the western countries in particular, but only because it falls close to the time of Christmas, and since Jewish parents and grandparents did not want their youngsters to feel deprived during the Christmas gift-giving season, Hanukkah's importance sort of became inflated. Not that it is insignificant, but most knowledgeable Jews would probably prefer that Jewish families give all the holidays the extraordinary attention that Hanukkah receives.

Hanukkah is often referred to as the Festival of Lights. It marks an event that took place in Jerusalem some 2,200 years ago. At that time the Syrian-Greco king Antiochus ruled the Jewish community of ancient Palestine and he sought to dissuade the Jews from worshiping God in their customary manner. This resulted in a revolt led by a man named Mattathias and his five heroic sons, who came to be known as *Maccabees* (Hebrew for hammerers), for they continued to battle against their oppressors until they succeeded in driving them out. When the Maccabees entered the Holy Temple in Jerusalem, they were shocked and saddened to find it desecrated; they set about cleansing it, and in the process found a small jug of specially prepared, ritually pure oil that looked as though it would last only for one day—miraculously, it continued to burn and shed light for eight days. That is why Hanukkah is celebrated for eight days, and one candle is lit on the first night, two on the second, and so on. The word *Hanukkah* means (in Hebrew) rededication, referring to the Holy Temple, and also acting as a reminder of the need to rededicate ourselves to good deeds and pure living.

Children especially enjoy Hanukkah since it has become a time for gift-giving. It is also a time when young and old play games with a *dreidel,* a spinning top marked with four letters, each of which stands for a Hebrew word: *nes gadol haya sham*—a great miracle occurred there.

In suburban America, one of the most inspiring sights is the season of Hanukkah and Christmas, when Jewish and Christian neighbors display their respective holiday symbols—the

Jews often place an electric candelabrum *(menorah)* in the window and add one light nightly during Hanukkah, while their Christian neighbors put up wreaths and other decorations.

In January there occurs a minor Jewish festival observed mostly in Israel and marked primarily by families closely identified with a synagogue. This is the lovely celebration known as *Tu B'Shvat,* meaning the fifteenth day of the Hebrew month Shvat, which is set aside as Jewish Arbor Day. On this day, which is sometimes also called New Year for Trees, young and old in Israel go out to the forests and fields and plant saplings, in the hope they will grow and become a boon to the country. In the west, families that mark this day usually make do with eating fruits that are indigenous to Israel, and also donate funds for trees to be planted in Israel.

Purim usually falls in February or March. This ancient festival marks the defeat of Haman, the evil prime minister of ancient Persia who wanted to kill all the Jews in the empire. This plot was overturned by the Jewish queen Esther, who persuaded her husband, King Ahaseurus, to rescind Haman's decree and to hang Haman and his cohorts instead. In the biblical tale, which is found in the scroll of Esther, the queen's uncle, Mordecai, also plays a key role.

On the eve of Purim, Jews usually gather in the synagogue to hear the reading of the Esther scroll, known as the *megilla.* Youngsters in the congregation come equipped with noisemakers, called *groggers,* and each time Haman's name is uttered, everybody shouts, stomps and twirls his grogger. It's a time for merrymaking, and traditionally it is even permissible to drink so much that "one cannot distinguish between Haman and Mordecai." Walking through the streets of Jerusalem on Purim eve and seeing young Hassidic Jews stumbling through the streets because they have imbibed too much—for religious reasons!—is an unforgettable experience. It is also customary on Purim to eat a special triangular Danish-like pastry filled with poppy seed or prune, called a *hamantash.*

The next major Jewish holiday is *Pesach* (Passover), which usually falls in April, sometimes in late March. This is the oldest of all Jewish holidays and recalls the exodus of the Israelite slaves from Egypt, more than three thousand years ago. It is also the most popularly celebrated of all Jewish holidays, according to most polls. In recent years, as the percentage of traditional Jewish families has declined, many synagogues and community centers have organized public seders—festive, religious dinners—for single-parent families, people who are divorced, widowed, or living alone. The seder is the center piece of the eight-day holiday (seven in Israel).

The *Haggadah,* which literally means the narrative, is read aloud ceremoniously at the seder and recounts the exodus of the Israelites, their forty-years trek to freedom in the Promised Land under the leadership of Moses. Each person at the table is encouraged to consider himself one of those slaves—so that he may better appreciate the value of freedom. The theme of freedom is the main thrust of the Passover celebration, although it, too, marks the season of first planting in Israel.

It is a holiday suffused with symbolism. *Matza,* unleavened bread, is eaten as a reminder of the Israelites' flight, when they could not wait for bread dough to rise. Traditional Jews use the pre-Passover period as a time to clean the house and cupboards thoroughly, to rid the home of *chametz,* or leaven. (There are many Jews, not necessarily Orthodox, who change all their cooking and serving utensils for the Passover period. In grocery stores, certain foods are designated "kosher for Passover"—that is, they are certified by a rabbi as being totally free of any leaven).

At the seder table it is customary to invite guests to share in the family's bounty. In recent years, many of these guests have been Soviet Jewish immigrants who in many instances had never before taken part in a seder. The various foods on the table represent Passover events: the *maror* (bitter herbs) represent the Israelite slaves' suffering; salt water recalls the tears shed by the Jewish people's ancestors when they were still

101

enslaved; the *charoset* (a mixture of wine, chopped nuts, cinnamon and apple) represents the mortar that the slaves used in their labors.

The seder plate in the center of the holiday table also contains a hard boiled egg and some roasted meat, symbolizing the ancient Israelites' dairy and meat sacrifices at the Holy Temple. There is also a green vegetable, known as *carpas,* that recalls the fact that it is spring, when new growth and new vegetation begin.

Traditionally, the youngest person at the seder table asks the Four Questions, to which the Haggadah is, in effect, a response. It is also traditional to drink four cups of wine, recalling God's promise to the Israelites, made four times, that He would liberate them from slavery.

Another seder custom is the spilling of wine to commemorate the ten plagues that eventually persuaded the Egyptians to allow the Israelites to depart. The *afikoman,* the final piece of matza shared by everyone after the meal, has become an opportunity for a youngster at the table to demand a "ransom" before he hands back the matza hidden by him at the start of the seder.

The entire Passover holiday and the seder itself are designed to bolster people's appreciation of liberty, and to reaffirm their faith in God and in the teachings of Judaism.

Jewish members of the United States armed forces have celebrated Passover seders on the high seas, in lonely outposts in Greenland, Iceland, Africa and elsewhere, and as guests of Jewish families residing near U.S. military or naval bases.

In the Nazi era, some Jews tried to celebrate Passover inside concentration camps, and to some extent they succeeded. Inmates of prisons today are usually afforded an opportunity to hold some kind of seder. Patients in hospitals and convalescent homes are also helped to commemorate the holiday.

The last major Jewish holiday in the Jewish calendar is *Shavuot,* known as the Feast of Weeks, which usually falls in late May or June. It both commemorates the Jewish people's receiving of the Torah at Mount Sinai, and also marks the first harvest of the season. It always follows Passover by seven weeks.

In a very real sense Shavuot is the birthday of the Torah, and recalls God's revelation at Sinai to Moses. Special prayers are recited on this holiday, singing God's praises. Most synagogues are bedecked with greens and flowers, pointing up the agricultural theme. In ancient days, it was customary for farming families to bring their first fruits to the temple at Jerusalem, to offer thanks to God for their good fortune. That is why Shavuot is also referred to as the Festival of First Fruits.

The traditional dish consumed on this holiday is cheese blintzes (dumplings filled with sweetened cream cheese)—a reminder of God's promise that Israel would be a land flowing with milk and honey.

Two other holidays should be mentioned: Israel Independence Day, which has been celebrated only since the establishment of Israel in 1948, and which usually falls in May. *Lag B'Omer*, which also falls in May, is a kind of half-festival that commemorates the Jews' struggle against the Romans.

The Jewish calendar also notes two other dates that cannot, however, be called holidays. The first is *Yom Hashoah*, a day commemorating the Holocaust, during which six million Jews were slaughtered. This is usually observed a few days after Passover (on the 27th of the Hebrew month Nissan); and *Tisha B'Av*, the ninth day of the month Av, a summer date that commemorates the destruction of both the first and second Holy Temples in Jerusalem, in the years 586 B.C.E. and 70 C.E. respectively.

In late summer, participants in early morning services in most synagogues can already hear, one month before Rosh Hashanah, the blast of the *shofar*, the ram's horn, reminding them that the new year is fast approaching and the time for repentance is at hand.

CHAPTER TEN
VIEWPOINTS AND ATTITUDES

ONE OF THE COMMON MISCONCEPTIONS ABOUT JUDAISM IS that it is a religion steeped in the past, emphasizing historic events and achievements while neglecting the contemporary world and its day-to-day problems.

This is actually far from the truth. Judaism lays heavy emphasis on the history of the Jewish people and of Judaism—but only in order to better understand the present, and to translate the lessons learned from historical experience into solutions for today's problems.

There are two groups of Jews, in particular, who share this misconception. Many ultra-Orthodox Jews insist on living today exactly as their great-grandfathers did many generations ago; they wear the same kind of clothes, head coverings and other articles, that were customary in seventeenth-century Poland, insisting that this paraphernalia is part and parcel of Judaism. To see a Hassid in hot summertime Jerusalem, perspiring profusely under a furred hat called a *shtreimel,* is to understand how religious faith can sometimes take a childish turn.

The other group that many Jews find irritating can best be classified as the nostalgic Jews—those who do not observe any religious laws, who are not committed to Jewish cultural life, and who are essentially divorced from any organized movements designed to help Israel, needy Jews, Jewish-sponsored hospitals and other social institutions, but who concentrate on evoking the Jewish celebrations they remember from their parents' or grandparents' day. These people are not only divorced from modern Jewish life, but they insist on portraying "Jewishness" as something that took place in the past. According to them, Jewish life was wonderful, wise and worthy of remembering—but it is now a thing of the past. These people, consciously or otherwise, have accepted the idea that Judaism, as the religious faith of a very tiny number of people in the world, must sooner or later die out.

This viewpoint is not unknown in Jewish history, and it is more widespread today than is generally acknowledged. In those progressive, enlightened countries where Jews are permitted to live freely and to practice their religious faith, there is widespread intermarriage and subsequent assimilation. In countries like Sweden, Denmark and Norway, for example, with relatively small Jewish populations, more than half of the Jews marry outside the Jewish community. This same percentage has reached the smaller, isolated Jewish communities of the United States and England.

The Jewish historian Cecil Roth once estimated that since the Jews are an ancient people, the world's Jewish population could easily have reached one hundred million were it not for massacres, forced conversions and expulsions—and intermarriage and assimilation.

Passive, nostalgic Jews may number as much as half of the world's Jewish population outside Israel. The only time they usually alter their view is during a period of emergency or danger. In 1967, when a coalition of Arab states led by

Egypt's Gamal Abdel Nasser threatened to overrun Israel and produce a second Holocaust, virtually every Jew in the world came forward to offer help and support. For a short period of time, nostalgia gave way to deep concern for the contemporary Jewish crisis. However, when there are no urgent crises confronting the Jewish community, substantial numbers of Jews sink back into passivity, convinced that Judaism is a thing of the past.

In actuality, Jewish theology stresses that life is to be lived here and now, and that an understanding of the past must lead to a better appreciation of how to conduct our lives in the present. The historian-philosopher Nathan Krochmal wrote, more than a century ago, that "the strength of Judaism consists of this—as soon as one period of history comes to an end, another begins. A new idea replaces the old, fresh forces come into play, and the result is continuous progress."

Another theme which is prevalent in Judaism is that life is unpredictable and must therefore never be taken for granted. Judaism, in other words, advises its adherents not to be complacent, not to be fatalistic, but to be alert every day, to see things realistically and wisely, to derive whatever moral lessons and wisdom we can from the past, but not to allow ourselves to sink into the past, either as individuals or as a community.

A study session in a synagogue can be a most inspiring scene. The students may be retired professors or physicians or accountants or taxi drivers, but when they meet at a Talmud class they seem to take on a new role—they often become animated by the discussion, expressing views and opinions, arguing one point against another. To an outsider, the subject matter may appear to be esoteric—what happens if a person's pet ruins the neighbor's garden? Who is responsible? Should compensation be paid?

After a while, it becomes clear that all the arguments, all the pilpulistic discussions, share one goal: to come up with a moral, just solution. In other words, to use precedents and previous arguments to arrive at correct and defensible solutions for today. Thus, a congregant in synagogue or a student of Talmud swiftly learns that all that he does and learns and absorbs should raise his life on earth to a higher plateau, to a more ethical lifestyle.

* * *

Since Judaism does not have a fixed statement of beliefs, people sometimes wonder about Judaism's views on a wide range of specific subjects. To arrive at these answers often requires years of study and experience. What follow are a number of Judaism's attitudes and views on various topics, accompanied by a cautionary note: chances are that some rabbis and commentators may look askance at these views, and offer interpretations of their own. To a neophyte this may at first seem confusing, but to anyone who makes a serious study of Judaism it will be perfectly normal. One must remember that in the Jewish community everyone is equal; every Jew must live his life as morally and as well as possible for when he appears before God there will be no intercessor—each person directly reports to God at the end of his life. Therefore, each person has the right to interpret, explain and comment on the Torah and the Jewish texts, bearing in mind that the rabbi holds that title by virtue of his or her greater knowledge and role as a teacher, but not as a supplicant for anyone, nor as a surrogate.

Perhaps that is why the confessional prayers recited on the High Holy Days are spoken aloud by a congregation which undoubtedly includes both sinners and saints—everyone comes before God together, as one community, and prays for joint forgiveness.

One of mankind's most impressive traits—pure altruism—is explained in the Talmud succinctly: "My father planted for me, and I plant for my children." Albert Einstein put it another way: "Only a life lived for others is life worthwhile." Closely allied with altruism are kindness and compassion. These two characteristics are sure signs of humanity. And all Jewish teaching is infused with the theme so beautifully expressed in the Bible, namely, that we humans are created "in the image of God," and therefore we must conduct ourselves accordingly. In addition, another theme is constantly referred to—above us all there is God, we humans are here on earth below, and somewhere between us are the angels. All of the teachings and regulations of Judaism are designed but for one purpose: to elevate people a little higher, toward the angels, and therefore closer to God.

A talmudic statement declares that the "Torah begins and ends with kindness—God clothing Adam and Eve, and burying Moses." One talmudic commentator noted that there is a subtle difference between kindness and charity: "Charity is limited to the living, the poor, and donating money; kindness also applies to the dead, the rich, and personal service."

In biblical days, Jews were admonished in the book of Proverbs: "Let not kindness and truth forsake you." And in the fourteenth century the commentator Aaron Halevi cautioned that "it is a duty to cultivate kindness." In this century, the Hebraist-novelist A. Kabak reminded his readers: "You have wells of kindness within your heart. At times man will bless you more for a smile, a kindly glance, a gesture of forgiveness, than for treasures of gold."

The Bible, the Talmud, and all the rabbinical commentaries and codes emphasize the vital importance of being charitable—to the poor, the widow and orphan, the sick and handicapped. Judaism stresses that this spirit of charitableness must be extended to Jews and Gentiles alike. The infrastructure of the organized Jewish community provides for vast sums to be donated voluntarily for the infirm, the ill, and for virtually anyone who needs a kindly, compassionate hand. In various periods, Jewish communities have imposed a tax on every family to provide funds for the less fortunate members of society. Today, in the United States and in most western countries philanthropic donations are usually voluntary, although solicitation is generally required to get most people to give.

Judaism has always regarded people through a prism of reality. Thus among the laws of charity found in Jewish texts is the warning that a man may not give if by so doing he neglects the well-being of his own family. Neither may a person impoverish himself by acts of charity. A person who seeks charitable aid from a social agency or a rabbi should be checked, Judaism advises, but this must be done with discretion and tact. However, if such a person asks for food because he is hungry, accept his statement and hand him the food. It is better that such a person receive food, even if it is suspected that his request may not be valid.

People should display a genuine love and concern for the poor in the community, Judaism teaches, but they must at the same time fight poverty and do everything possible to abolish it. A person's life should be graced with happiness, dignity, fulfillment and prosperity—and none of these goals is attainable if poverty looms large. Therefore, Judaism teaches, we must succor the poor, and battle against poverty.

*　*　*

Judaism is sometimes characterized as a sober, even sad-faced, religion. Nothing could be further from the truth! Jews who make such claims speak from the fact that they enter a synagogue only on the High Holy Days, usually for a short period of time, and notice that people look somber, worried, serious, and therefore Judaism is divorced from joyfulness and happiness. American Jews, in particular, reared to believe in the credo of "life, liberty and the pursuit of happiness" sometimes use the excuse that Judaism is too serious for them.

In truth, Judaism celebrates life and good times, and wants everyone to enjoy life on earth. There is a story told of the righteous man, a veritable *tsadik,* who died and went to heaven, fully expecting to enjoy his reward in Eden. After all, he knew that he had obeyed most of the traditional 613 religious commandments, he had never sinned, never missed synagogue services, gave charity, and was a respectable member of the community. When he got to heaven he was shocked to learn that he would not be allowed to enter. "Why?" he demanded. Because, the angelic authorities replied, you did not take time out to enjoy life enough. That too is a vital *mitzvah,* a religious duty.

Judaism does not say that people should pursue happiness, but instead postulates that if they do certain deeds, happiness will find them. For example, someone who trusts in God, or does not transgress, or who supports wisdom, or does not come into contact with evil people, or who practices justice, or who is considerate of the poor, or who keeps the Sabbath, or who earns a living by honest labor—all these people are happy. Happiness is seen in Judaism as an ideal state, but one that cannot consciously be sought out. It will come, if a person lives a truly religious life, which will bring not only happiness but also serenity, fulfillment and inner joy.

Judaism is sometimes charged with being a harsh religion that treats the concept of love superficially. On the contrary, a religious Jew recites the basic prayer of Judaism twice daily: "And you shall love the Lord your God with all your heart and with all your soul, and with all your might." In Leviticus we are told clearly: "You shall love your neighbor as yourself." Judaism stresses family love, between parents and children, and between husband and wife.

There is also in Judaism an almost mystical quest of love for God. Many have interpreted the Song of Songs, part of the Bible, not as a love poem in which a man and a woman serenade each other, but a disguised poem of the love of the Jewish people for God. The great philosopher Maimonides, who has always been considered a leading rationalist, sounded almost mystical when he wrote:

"When man loves God with a love that is fitting, he automatically carries out all the precepts in love. What is the love that is fitting? It is that man should love God with an ex-

111

traordinary powerful love to the extent that his soul becomes tied to the love of God, and he longs for it all the time.

"It is as if he were love-sick, unable to get the woman he loves out of his mind, pining for her constantly when he sits or stands, when he eats and drinks. Even more than this is the love of God in the hearts of those who love Him and yearn constantly for Him, as He has commanded us, 'with all your heart and all your soul.'"

A sixteenth-century mystic, Moses Cordovero, taught that "a man should . . . honor all creatures in whom he recognizes the exalted nature of the Creator . . . and he should bring the love of his fellow men into his heart, even loving the wicked as if they were his brothers, saying, 'Would that these were righteous, returning in repentance.'"

As for marital love, the ideal in Judaism is the love that Adam and Eve enjoyed while they were in the Garden of Eden. A talmudic scholar urges that a man should love his wife as much as he loves himself, and should respect her more than himself.

The Hassidic master Levi Yitzhok taught that "whether a man really loves God can be determined by the love he bears toward his fellow men." A talmudic scholar said: "Teach not the love of scholars only, but the love of all." The late rabbi Leo Baeck, who survived a Nazi concentration camp, said: "The most touching chapter about love of the enemy is contained in the history of the Jewish people. No wrong, no physical violence, have availed to stifle the human love in their hearts."

While stressing the importance of romantic love between husband and wife, Jewish tradition remains sharply realistic. A Yiddish proverb says: "Love tastes sweet, but only with bread." And in the Talmud there is a passage that reads: "When love was strong we could have made our bed on a sword's blade, but now when it is weak, a bed of sixty cubits is not large enough for us."

* * *

Judaism stresses the vital importance of respecting the elderly. The Bible says straightforwardly: "Rise up before the hoary head, and honor the face of the old man." The strong tradition in Judaism that advocates caring for the aged is expressed in the ancient words of the psalmist: "Cast me not off in the time of old age, when my strength fails, forsake me not." The prophet Isaiah, describing a generation of Jews that was corrupt and evil, noted that "the child shall behave insolently against the aged, and the base against the honorable."

Every Jewish community in the world supports institutions that will enable elderly members to live out their final years in dignity and comfort. Essentially, caring for the aged is seen in Judaism as nothing more than—and nothing less than—an extension of the fifth of the Ten Commandments: "Honor your father and your mother, that your days may be long upon the land which the Lord your God gives you."

In the final years of the twentieth century, especially in industrialized nations like the United States, there has surfaced a growing phenomenon that was not too well-known a few generations ago. People find themselves alienated one from another, and this can include parents and children, siblings, relatives, neighbors. The egocentric philosophy of "me'ism" seems to have found a home in the cruel concept of alienation and loneliness. People seem to withdraw into their own, tiny, self-centered worlds, and suffer from feelings of being cut off—from family, friends, community—and from the cruelty of loneliness. A long time ago Judaism recognized the threat of such a development, and told Jews in no uncertain terms: "Do not separate yourself from the community." This is a fundamental teaching that recognizes people's innate need for companionship, and for social support.

A Jew who belongs to a synagogue finds that even if he has a small family, and a small circle of personal friends, his congregational membership gives him a comforting feeling of an extended family. Typically, a parent celebrating the birth of a child, or a child's bar or bat mitzvah, or a wedding, or a

113

grandchild's birth, will discover that fellow congregants—even people he may not know well, or people he is not especially fond of—will extend congratulations and good wishes. Such a person, in all likelihood, will not be troubled by loneliness or alienation.

In a time of personal tragedy, such support from the extended family of congregants can be of enormous healing value to a mourner. A person sitting at home in the first seven days (the *shiva* period) of mourning derives comfort and strength from visitors who understand his profound sense of loss.

In some cases, when Jewish families are not regular synagogue members, membership in a Jewish organization often substitutes for the concept of the synagogue's extended family. Women especially, who devote considerable time and effort to advancing the work of women's organizations, find that their friendships are rewarded in time of joy and in time of need by the supportive action of fellow members.

Perhaps the following true story illustrates the point best:

Two brothers and a sister survived the Holocaust and immigrated to the United States. None of them ever married, and they shared an apartment in New York. The brothers opened a small business together, which after a time prospered; the sister cooked and kept house for them. They had lost their parents, aunts, uncles and cousins in the Holocaust and found it very difficult to make new friends in the United States. The two brothers met new people every day in their work; the sister, alone in the apartment, was a virtual recluse. Hardly a word was ever exchanged with neighbors. This was their life for some twenty years, and the inevitable happened: after nearly two decades of alienation and painful loneliness, the sister began to show serious signs of emotional disturbance. She became depressed, and the brothers did not know what to do.

A distant relative who had also survived the Holocaust now lived in Israel and urged that the three come for a visit. They did so, and discovered almost instantaneously that life in Israel was very different—it was largely lived physically outdoors, in the street and on the balconies that graced every home. And people talked to one another, opening up to each other and allowing the listener to respond in kind. Within a matter of days, the spinster sister was smiling, talking; her brothers saw the immediate transformation and decided to sell their business at once and emigrate to Israel.

It is not unusual for strangers in a synagogue to be approached by a congregant, who will try to make them feel welcome. Strangers who attend a synagogue service, and then sip some wine or bite into a piece of cake at a post-service *kiddush* together with regular worshipers, do not remain strangers for long.

When large waves of Jewish immigrants came to America in the years before World War I, they formed *landsmanshaften,* mutual help societies designed to offer support as they adjusted to their new lives. These groups played a very important role by providing financial help, medical care, guidance about schooling and citizenship lessons, employment, and other vital issues. And of course they gave each member-family a sense of belonging, of community. In Jewish teaching, alienation from the Jewish community—whether it is accidental or deliberate—is a rejection of Judaism. On the obverse of the coin, membership in a synagogue or in a Jewish organization is a clear declaration of belonging and affiliation.

* * *

One of the greatest Jewish sages of all time was Hillel, for whom the B'nai B'rith-sponsored Jewish student centers on college campuses are named. Hillel taught:

"Do not be sure of yourself until the day of your death.

"Do not judge a fellow human being, until you are in his situation.

"Do not say, 'When I have free time, I will study'—for you may never have free time.

115

"An ignorant person cannot be fearful of sin.

"An ignorant person cannot be pious.

"A bashful person cannot learn.

"A short-tempered person cannot teach.

"Not everyone busy in business learns wisdom.

"Wherever there are no worthy people, you try to be a real person.

"More flesh, more worms. More possessions, more worries.

"More good deeds, more peace."

Hillel's axioms are contained in *Ethics of the Fathers*, a text that is often found in the *siddur*, the Jewish prayerbook. Many other sagacious teachers are cited. Rabbi Jochanan ben Zakai, for example, once posed the following question to five of his rabbinical students: "What kind of lifestyle should one strive to follow?" One rabbi answered that a person should have a generous eye. Another replied that one should find a good friend. The third said that a person should seek out a good neighbor. The fourth student replied that a person should develop foresight. The fifth rabbi, Elazar ben Arakh, said that one should have a generous heart. At this their teacher responded: "I prefer Elazar ben Arakh's answer, for it includes all the others."

Rabbi Yehoshua is quoted in *Ethics of the Fathers* as teaching that three things will ruin a person's life: "A begrudging eye, the evil impulse, and hatred of one's fellow human beings."

Another rabbi, Akiva, taught that "everything is foreseen, yet freedom of choice has been given. The world is judged favorably but everything depends on the quantity of good deeds." Rabbi ben Zoma said: "Who is wise? He who learns from all people." He also said: "Who is strong? He who conquers his evil impulse. Who is honored? He who honors his fellow human beings."

* * *

One of the vilest sins, strongly condemned in Jewish tradition, is slander. A talmudic passage declares that the "penalty for slander equals that of all the cardinal sins." A slanderer, Judaism teaches, harms three people—the person he is talking about, the person to whom he is telling his slander, and himself. One commentator explained God's decisions not to allow Moses to enter the Promised Land as a punishment for having denounced the Israelites as "rebels" during their forty-year wanderings in the wasteland.

On the other hand, shame—that is, being ashamed of one's misdeeds—is seen in Judaism as being a positive trait. A talmudic sage said that Jerusalem "was destroyed because its people had no shame." Another talmudist taught that "if one is ashamed of a sin, all his sins are forgiven." And a Yiddish proverb notes that "where there's no shame before men, there's no fear of God." In the eleventh century, the poet-scholar Shlomo ibn-G'virol taught that the "greatest of all virtues is a sense of shame."

Since Judaism proclaims that man was created in God's image, it stands to reason that every adherent of the Jewish faith must possess a sense of self-esteem. The twentieth-century philosopher Martin Buber cautioned that "without being and remaining oneself, there is no love." The great Hillel, two millenia ago, advised: "If I am not for myself, who will be? But if I am only for myself, what am I?"

Ten enemies, a Yiddish axiom asserts, cannot harm a man as much as he can harm himself. Sholom Aleichem used to say: "No tongue speaks as much ill of us, as does our own." While Jewish tradition acknowledges the need for self-esteem and the need for every person to genuinely feel a sense of self-worth, it also cautions against arrogance, pride and—self-contempt.

Throughout Jewish history there have been a small number who manifested a Jewish self-hatred. Those who did not succeed in life blamed their failure on having been born Jewish, i.e., belonging to a minority religious group. Some took the logical step and converted to the majority religion surrounding them. Some, both those who converted and those who did not, went through life cursing their Jewish origins. Some, even after converting to another faith (almost always Christianity), continued to feel a sense of community with the Jewish people.

By and large, Judaism dismisses people who abandon the Jewish community and then turn against it. From bitter experience, most Jews know that Christians generally respect Jews who uphold their faith and show contempt for Jews (or ex-Jews) who malign Judaism. A long time ago a talmudic wit commented thus on self-hating Jews and ex-Jews: "Three hate their own kind—dogs, roosters, and prostitutes."

Thus, Judaism encourages people to develop a sense of self-worth, of self-respect, of self-control, of self-confidence—but abhors any inclination to self-contempt. What is needed in the world, Judaism seems to be saying, is an ambience of love for all creatures, for when all is said and done, God created everyone and everything, and He did this with love and compassion, and not with hatred and anger.

On the other hand, Jewish teaching also warns people against a life of self-centeredness and selfishness. The founder of the Hassidic movement, the Baal Shem Tov, said that "there is no room for God in a person who is full of himself." A thousand years ago Maimonides taught: "An ignorant man believes the entire universe exists only for himself. So, if anything unexpected happens to him, he concludes that the whole world is an evil place." Israel Zangwill, the modern British author, put it another way: "Selfishness is the only real atheism. Hopefulness, unselfishness are the only true religion."

* * *

A problem that rabbis speak of fairly often is centered around the synagogue service. Congregants and non-members alike sometimes admit that they find the rote recitation of the prayers a difficult chore. "I don't understand the Hebrew

118

words," a congregant may tell the rabbi, "and when I turn to the English translation, it doesn't quite do it for me."

Other complaints around this same theme include: "What does God need my words of praise for?"; or, that the repetition of the same words, week in and week out, year in and year out, becomes boring. In the closing years of the twentieth century, many Jews find it hard to offer hymns of praise to God—in a world of war, disease, poverty, evil.

This is not a new problem in the long history of the Jewish people. Scholars, rabbis and sages have wrestled with this issue and have come up with some interesting recommendations. Rabbi Leo Baeck said that "the purpose of prayer is to leave us alone with God." A talmudic passage states: "God longs for the prayer of the righteous." The late chief rabbi of pre-Israel Palestine, Abraham Kook, believed that "by prayer, we raise ourselves to a world of perfection." Claude Montefiore made an important distinction when he wrote, at the turn of the twentieth century, "to pray is not the same as to pray for." Samson Raphael Hirsch, in 1836, said: "The aim of our worship is the purification, enlightenment, and uplifting of our inner selves."

Some people find that, rather than struggle to understand the full meaning of the words of the prayers, they prefer to listen to the sound of the ancient Hebrew phrases—the musical chanting of the cantor, the rhythmic reading of the Torah scroll, the sometimes mystical tones of the Hebrew syllables. They all combine to create an atmosphere of holiness, and connection to four thousand years of Jewish history, and to Judaism and the Jewish people in every nook and corner of the world.

Rabbi Abraham J. Heschel said that prayer—in a synagogue, in a community, a congregation—can bring in its wake a sense of "spiritual security." He said: "We need witnesses, human beings who are engaged in worship, who for a moment sense the truth that life is meaningless without at-

119

tachment to God." He added that a synagogue is a place where people learn "the insights of the spirit," and experience "inner silence," and can learn, for a brief time at least, to "be still."

Judaism therefore regards prayer as an answer to people who sense "spiritual unease." Prayer in Judaism is an expression of gratitude, for Jewish teaching strongly cautions against taking life or its blessings for granted. Prayer is also seen as a regular restatement of a commitment to a life dedicated to ethical living, to compassion and justice. Prayer provides an opportunity for worshipers to feel close to God, and to develop hope and confidence for the future.

The German-Jewish poet Heinrich Heine wrote: "God created man to admire the splendor of the world. Every author desires the praise of his work."

CHAPTER ELEVEN
CHOOSE LIFE

ABOVE ALL ELSE, JUDAISM IS A TOTALLY LIFE-ORIENTED commitment. What does a Jew say when he raises his glass in a toast? *L'chayim!* To life!

Judaism firmly believes that life, with all its problems, obstacles and disappointments, is well worth living. Cynicism, pessimism and negativism are completely alien concepts. The Jewish religion, the Jewish way of life, notwithstanding centuries of oppression, are based on hope and optimism. Israelis may recount a long list of their country's problems—threats from the Arabs, a lack of raw materials, insufficient water resources, serious squabbling between religious and secular compatriots; and then, almost magically, they will laugh and add, *yi'hi'ye tov*—it'll be okay. Judaism's optimism has been absorbed into the very fabric of modern Israel.

There is a beautiful midrashic tale that bears repeating. In the course of its history, the midrash says, the Jewish people sang ten psalms, as recorded in the Bible. First, when the Israelites were liberated from Egyptian slavery. Second, the song of triumph, following the successful crossing of the Red Sea. Third, when the Israelites were in the wilderness and a well appeared and provided them with water. Fourth, the song that Moses offered before he died. Fifth, Joshua's song of praise and thanks following his victory over the Amorite kings. Sixth, Deborah's and Barak's song, following the defeat of Sisera. Seventh, David's song, following his deliverance from his enemies. Eighth, the song offered by Solomon at the dedication of the Holy Temple. Ninth, the song of Jehoshafat as he set out to fight the Moabites and the Ammonites. And the tenth is the great psalm that the Jewish people sang, and will sing to the end of days, when they will be granted everlasting deliverance.

Essentially Judaism has always believed in the eventual victory of right over might, and in the eternal survival of the Jewish people.

It is therefore not difficult to understand why there are many Jews today who see behind the reestablishment of Israel the mystical hand of God. The sense of powerlessness that pervaded the world's Jewish communities in the 1930s and 1940s has yielded dramatically to a new sense of powerfulness, confidence and purpose in the development of Israel. No wonder so many prayerbooks have since added a prayer that speaks of Israel as a "promise of redemption." The despair and tragedy of the Holocaust period have been supplanted by an Israel that reflects hope and confidence in Judaism and the Jewish people, and this has bolstered the Jewish community immeasurably.

* * *

Significantly, the Israeli national anthem—and the theme song of the Jewish people worldwide, sung at dinners, conferences and the like—is titled *Hatikvah,* the hope. The song restates a basic Jewish maxim—hope will never die, we will always continue to believe in the future well-being of the Jewish people, and of its return to Zion and Jerusalem.

When the first pitiful survivors of the Holocaust emerged from the Nazi concentration camps, they were broken in body and spirit. Few people at first knew how to speak to them, how to reach them, how to try to reconnect them to humanity, and to the Jewish people; until one of the survivors himself spoke up, his voice quavering and weak. In Yiddish he said, *men tor nisht mis'ya'esh zein!* We dare not become discouraged!

The Talmud teaches that "as long as there is life, there is hope."

* * *

An old Yiddish refrain says, *siz shver tsu zein a yid*—it's hard to be a Jew. From the beginning it has been a tough struggle to continue to be Jewish. The early Israelites were slaves, they had to fight for every inch of soil in the Promised Land. For nearly fifteen hundred years the Jews had to battle against a pagan world anxious to snuff out this new religion that insisted on belief in one God, and that demanded strict ethical behavior. The small Jewish community of that era was isolated, but the Jews resisted because they had faith—and hope.

In the last two millenia, this same minuscule Jewish people was assaulted by vast empires, by powerful Christian and Moslem bodies—assaults that culminated in the obscenity of the Holocaust. Through the centuries the Jewish people, and Judaism, have suffered degradation, expulsion, massacre, and the violent hatred of mobs and their rulers. That the Jews remained hopeful and full of faith is a miracle, and at the same time a tribute to their inner spiritual strength.

Their strength came from a deeply-held faith in God, in the rightness of their faith, in the eventual triumph of goodness over evil. There were times when Jews believed that they had been singled out by God to spread His teachings through the world, and that their special chosenness by God carried with it the added onus of suffering. And there were also times when Jews believed that they themselves had been sinful, and their suffering and wandering was a punishment for their misdeeds.

Thus, Jews found themselves always hoping—for deliverance and redemption, and for repentance and forgiveness. One of the most moving moments in the Yom Kippur liturgy—on a day when everyone in synagogue is fasting, praying and hoping for a good year to come—occurs when the congregation together asks God for forgiveness and pardon. The prayer usually concludes on a hopeful, upbeat melodic refrain, in which everyone sings in one voice, "Forgive us, Pardon us, Grant us atonement."

* * *

Judaism strongly believes that although the world is far from perfect, it can be improved. What is more, Judaism teaches that in a very real sense we human beings are co-creators with God of the world, and therefore that it is our duty to help Him perfect it. Known as *tikun olam,* this is a fundamental Jewish concept. Many historians and political analysts have concluded that one of the reasons that Jews often seem to predominate in various movements to advance social justice and human welfare is because of this principle of *tikun olam*—which ironically is frequently found among non-practicing, as well as among committed, Jews.

Judaism, however, is not Pollyanna-ish. Sternly, realistically, the Jewish religion looks around the world and sees hatred, lust, greed, exploitation, injustice, poverty—and announces that these evils can and must be overcome. The Bible recounts that God created the world out of chaos, and Judaism in effect says we dare not let the world slip back into *tohu va'vahu,* into the anarchy and chaos from whence it came.

The pessimistic philosopher Schopenhauer believed that "optimism is not reconcilable with Christianity, and with Buddhism." Then he added: "The fundamental characteristics of Judaism are optimism and realism."

* * *

Judaism, many people claim, is obsessed with time. The Bible opens with the story of the creation of the world, in six days. There is a time to laugh, and a time to mourn, the Bible teaches. An observant Jew must always know the time, so that he can pray at a given time. The candles on Sabbath or holiday eve must be kindled at a given hour. And yet, Judaism says that a person's life should not be measured by time—longevity is not the criteria of a good, successful life; only life is to be measured by good deeds.

Judaism, then, does not measure a person's years, and it certainly does not take into account the accumulation of wealth. A wise person must develop pity for those who go through life seeking to accumulate jewels, big houses, cars, in the totally false belief that these material possessions will bring in their wake happiness, inner peace, true fulfillment. Jewish tradition does not accept asceticism as a way of life, but it seeks to make the point that a person needs only a limited amount of food, clothing and shelter in order to live comfortably.

If Judaism disdains a person's longevity or material possessions, then does it encourage happiness as the ultimate goal of human existence? Actually, yes and no—Judaism encourages people to be happy, to be happy with their lot in life, to enjoy each day, to spread joy; but it also recognizes that no one can go through life constantly smiling or laughing, any more than a person who loves golf can play the game all the time, or someone who loves singing can be expected to raise his voice in song all the time.

Judaism teaches that every person must continually grow— in learning, understanding, wisdom. All life is growth, Abba Hillel Silver taught, adding: "The splendor and miracle of the universe are growth, unfoldment, becoming—the life-seed passing through the dark mysterious stations of death and resurrection, until it breaks forth into the breathless glory of flower and fruit . . . Everything is a growing and a becoming. Nothing is done. Nothing is ended. Stars grow, planets grow, worlds grow. Throughout all creation is an unceasing, throbbing life which manifests itself endlessly in endless variety."

Living, in the Jewish tradition, is a constant intellectual

exercise and challenge. We need new ideas, new knowledge, new insight, all of which will enable us to grow wiser, more understanding, more human. And just as children experience growing pains, there are growing pains involved in attaining new intellectual, spiritual heights. Ergo, a Jew accepts this spiritual burden, confident that his determination to learn constantly, to have an open mind and an open heart, will in time elevate him to new plateaus of spirituality and everlasting peace.

* * *

To understand Judaism's drive toward an ethical life one must look back at its earliest years. In ancient times—nearly four thousand years ago—in the tiny land today called Israel that lies at the crossroads of Asia, Europe and Africa, there arose a new kind of man—a prophet. The prophets of old were the basic builders of the early forms of Judaism, and their teachings have had a marked influence over both Christianity and Islam.

These inspired men were not exactly rabbis or theologians, as we understand those terms today. They envisaged an ideal way of life for mankind, and preached that it was the best way to understand God, to come close to Him, and to rise to a higher level of human existence. They spoke from knowledge of their small people's unique history, and of the basic Torah teachings. One must bear in mind that the books of the Bible as we know them today were not gathered and organized until two thousand years after Moses, and it was only a thousand years later that Jewish religious philosophers even began to try to codify Jewish teaching and theology. The prophets preached, taught and admonished before the formal compilation of the Bible and of course the Talmud

Recent interpreters of Judaism have used a wide variety of western philosophies to expound on Judaism. Judaism did not oppose this trend, contending that whatever helped to clarify the religion was an acceptable aid toward understanding and appreciating it. However, Jewish scholars have never tried to equate any other religious outlook with Judaism, insisting that, divinely-inspired and prophetic, Judaism is completely unique.

In the computer age there are many people who undoubtedly would like to discover Judaism's program—they would like to read a neat, precise analysis defining it conclusively. In actuality, one must absorb Judaism slowly and let its insights, wisdom, tenets, traditions, hopes, expectations become part and parcel of one's life, bearing in mind that study must be continued at all times, that the Sabbath and holidays must be observed and enjoyed, that *mitzvot*—religious commandments, or good deeds as some prefer to call them—must be performed, and that one should not be afraid to question a teacher or a rabbi on a point of law or a point of view. Traditionally, Judaism has not asked Jews to blindly follow its rules and regulations, but rather, to follow and obey them, and yet question them when necessary.

Hovering above the details of Jewish life—at home, in the synagogue, in the world at large—is the over-arching principle, of which all people are constantly being reminded, that paramount in Judaism is the need to be compassionate, just, and ethical. A beautiful midrashic tale illustrates the point:

When the Israelites fleeing the bondage of Egypt crossed through the Red Sea on dry land because the waters had miraculously opened, God's angels rejoiced and expressed their glee that the pursuing Egyptians were drowned en masse. At this point God remonstrated with his angels: "Why do you rejoice?" He demanded. "The Egyptians are also human beings, and their death in the Red Sea is a time for mourning, not rejoicing."

Similarly, at the Passover seder table, when the *Haggadah* (holiday narrative) recounts the ten plagues that finally persuaded the pharoah to let the Israelites go free, it is customary to spill a drop of wine for each of the plagues—symbolically diminishing our own rejoicing and acknowledging the Egyptians' fate.

In the Jewish view, not all of humanity's darkened corners can be illumined, but enough light can be cast into them to make a difference. There is, in other words, a light at the end of the tunnel, where life will be near-perfect; and while we are walking through the tunnel we must throw as much light around as possible, and always keep our eyes on the bright, clear light that beckons us from afar. As one rabbi put it: nobody can possess a clear knowledge of God, but everyone can worship God with sincerity and devotion.

When a Jew awakens in the morning he is expected to recite an early morning prayer which includes the phrase: "The beginning of wisdom is fear [or, reverence] of God." This reverence, in Jewish tradition, is achieved through a person's behavior, through acts of loving-kindness, and through a life characterized by ethical conduct. Pragmatic Judaism says in effect, who needs theological speculation? What is needed is action, deeds; what the Yiddish so aptly terms *tachlis*—brass tacks.

The Bible speaks frequently of "knowing God," a phrase that is almost always interpreted to mean that if one conducts oneself in an ethical manner, knowledge of God will follow. In Judaism there are no secret codes, myths, beliefs, practices that purportedly will lead to happiness or salvation. Sharply, Judaism states that only by following certain prescribed paths, obeying the statutes, will a just society be established here on earth—and this in turn will bring on happiness and redemption.

Historical development, in the Jewish view, is not haphazard. There is a pattern in history that needs to be understood, and its lessons applied to the world around us. This pattern demonstrates that eventually goodness will emerge triumphant, for that is God's will, but—mankind must help propel this triumph forward.

Through the centuries thoughtful observers have distinguished differences between the ancient Greek and Jewish outlooks on life—the former concentrated on art, science and philosophy, while the latter concentrated on religion and morality. The Jewish perspective is that life and the physical world presents a changing, dynamic challenge, while the Greek view is static, and always seeks harmony in nature. The ancient Greeks stressed the need for rest, self-control, beauty and harmony, while the ancient Jewish prophets called for a passionate, vibrant and strong response to life's challenges. Judaism achieved remarkably prescient insights into human spiritual needs—insights that have remained true through all the ages.

Certain religions teach that people are not free to choose their path in life, that all is preordained and inevitable, and that while some people are chosen for eternal life, others are not. Conversely, these faiths assert that a man's meritorious deeds are of no consequence—everything is predetermined.

This is a view that Judaism rejects forcefully. People are created in the image of God and are free to choose a way of life, Judaism says. People can be moral or not, as they themselves—through their actions—determine. The Bible states that God says to the Jews: "See, I have set before you this day life and good, death and evil . . . therefore, choose life!"

* * *

In its optimistic mode, Judaism believes that mankind continues to move forward, developing more knowledge and a better world, despite the many backward, discouraging steps. Look around you, Jewish teaching says: living standards, for more and more people, are better than they were a century or two ago; educational opportunities are more widespread; health care is more attainable. Progress is slow, but still there seems to be a definite upward spiral in history. Perhaps it is true that people will never know "ultimate answers" about God, but does that really matter? If a person can have faith in

God, and find satisfaction in daily life, in work, in family, in society, he is bound to achieve a high measure of inner fulfillment. Sitting around, waiting for a revelation that will prove conclusively that God exists, is seen in Judaism as childish. A person must either make a "leap of faith," or accept a limited faith, and hope that in time—by pursuing a good lifestyle—a deeper sense of religious conviction will ensue.

In the ringing words of Rabbi Abba Hillel Silver: "Judaism admonished men not to despair of the future, nor of their own strength, nor of mankind's inexhaustible spiritual resources, nor of God's cooperation. Long and hard is the way, but there is a way, and there is a goal, and the faithful children of light will follow it and will not grow weary."

CHAPTER TWELVE
LOOKING AHEAD

PRIOR TO THE EXILE IMPOSED ON THEM BY THE ROMANS
nearly two thousand years ago, the Jews regarded themselves
as a full-fledged nation with a country of their own, a distinct
culture, an impressive history. In addition, this small Jewish
nation had one special feature that particularly set them off
from the rest of the world—their religious faith, which was
always a minority way of life.

After the Jews' expulsion from their homeland they gradually scattered to practically every corner of the world. For a
time there was a well-established Jewish community in
Babylonia, whose scholarship produced one of the great religious and literary treasures of mankind, the Babylonian Talmud. At another juncture in history, a Jewish community
thrived in Spain, creating what has come to be known as a
Golden Age, when immortal Hebrew liturgical poetry and
philosophical works were composed; this too came to a sud-
den and violent end when the Jews were expelled from the
Iberian peninsula in the fifteenth century. Jews prospered in
western Europe, in central Europe, in the Balkans, in Moslem
countries, and in recent centuries, in the western hemisphere.

Their earlier concept of themselves as a nation changed over the centuries, inasmuch as they no longer enjoyed political independence; over the years, the Jews' view of themselves gradually metamorphosed. Exiled, living in other peoples' lands, existing on sufferance, always fearful of violence from easily aroused mobs or harsh rulers, the Jews began to regard themselves primarily as a religious community. It is true that they never forgot their ancestral homeland. The Jewish prayerbook is filled with hopes for their return to Judea; most of the Jewish holidays reflect the homeland's seasonal life; at the conclusion of the Passover seder and the Yom Kippur service, everyone calls out, *L'shana ha'ba'a b'yeroosha'layeem!*—Next year in Jerusalem!

Nevertheless, as the centuries of exile mounted, and as Jews labored to adapt themselves to new surroundings, the idea of Jewish nationhood gave way to Jewish peoplehood and religious community. It was not until late in the nineteenth century, when the Zionist movement began in earnest, that Jews found themselves wondering what they were—an exiled nation, a religious faith, a people-cum-a-religious faith? It was always clear to Jews that no matter where they lived, they owed their political allegiance to their country of domicile. During World War I, for example, there were German and Austrian Jews fighting on one side of the war against British, French and American Jews. These were, after all, citizens of various countries, who happened to be Jewish.

Among thoughtful, insightful Jews living in western countries, the closing years of the twentieth century have seen agonizing new self-appraisals. After visiting Israel, many of these western Jews find themselves less satisfied with a self-definition which indicates they are members of a religious community, or a "people." Perhaps for the first time they sense that they also have a strong attachment to the people of Israel who, after all, are fellow Jews, and who have recreated the ancient Jewish homeland. In other words, the existence of Israel in the latter half of the twentieth century has bolstered the identity of Jews overseas, and has strengthened their commitment to Judaism—and at the same time, has left some with a gnawing question as to where they truly belong: as a small minority in a western country, or as part of the Jewish majority in Israel. No doubt this dilemma will persist for many years to come. Altogether, no more than 60,000 American Jews—about one percent of the total—have emigrated to Israel. The percentages in some western countries are slightly higher.

* * *

Does Judaism have a mission to convert the Gentiles? And if not, why not?

Christianity and Islam unashamedly proclaim that they have a mission to convert people to their respective faiths. Nonbelievers in various parts of the world are courted by Christian missionaries, who offer medical help, educational programs and other inducements, believing that their proselytizing is God's will. No doubt a number of these missionaries have raised the living standards of many people in far-off places.

Islam, over the centuries, has taken a different tack. Instead of persuasive means, its adherents have on occasion compelled whole peoples and countries to adopt the Moslem faith. In Iran, which is Moslem but not Arab, a whole Jewish community in the nineteenth century was forcibly converted to Islam—under penalty of death.

Judaism is not a proselytizing faith. This is not a sign of arrogance. Firstly, Judaism respects all other religious faiths, especially Christianity and Islam which share a monotheistic belief. Secondly, those who wish to become Jews are cautioned that this is not a simple decision, that it is sometimes burdensome, and that their motivation should be based on true conviction arising from a period of intense study.

When such a person is accepted for conversion, their status is virtually equal to that of a Jew who was born of a Jewish mother. The conversion ceremony is simple and swift; in an Orthodox conversion a Gentile man has to undergo at least a symbolic circumcision. There are estimates that, in recent years, some ten thousand Americans have been converting to Judaism annually and many of these people—a greater proportion of converts are women than men—become actively involved with synagogues, Jewish organizations and other communal programs. The number of Jews in the United States who intermarry with Gentiles and fall away from the Jewish community through assimilation is a moot statistic, but it is believed to be substantially higher than the number of "Jews by choice," as the former Gentiles like to be called.

* * *

Does Judaism believe in the hereafter? The Bible makes no mention of heaven or hell, and in the early biblical period there was almost no concern with this issue. Gradually, however, over the years and under the influence of various host cultures, Judaism began to take on some thoughts about life after death.

It is, to this day, a rather murky area. Some Jewish texts and some of our greatest rabbis have written about the "world to come," strongly indicating that after death another, very good universe is especially reserved for good people. Other interpreters and religious scholars have taught that only the soul lives on after death, and some mystical traditions hold that all the souls will, in the messianic era, finally assemble in Jerusalem. In addition, there are some Jews who believe in the concept of *techiyat ha'meteem,* or resurrection. The Reform Judaism movement formally rejects this, although it accepts the idea of the soul's immortality. Given Judaism's emphasis on life in the present, probably a large percentage of the Jewish people tends not to think about such issues at all. If after death they will enter an Eden, that's great. And if they are resurrected, that's even better. Perhaps only among the ultra-Orthodox Jews is there a firm belief in the chance of resurrection and a heavenly abode.

The great Maimonides, a rationalist and a physician as well

as a rabbi, apparently did believe in the "world to come," but he described it as a place in which there are neither bodies nor bodily forms but only the disembodied souls of the righteous who have become like ministering angels. Since there are no bodies, there is no eating or drinking there, nor is there anything which the human body needs in this world.

Certain rabbis have apparently given the matter much thought. Many years ago they wrote that the world to come will feature a time that "is all Sabbath," and that the "heavenly academy" will feature God teaching the Torah to the righteous. Jewish mystics have always emphasized that this world is only a preparation for the next, and that if man leads a good life on earth, he will earn a place in the next world, there to enjoy the "true life."

* * *

All through the centuries, there has been a tug of war within Judaism over one issue—which is more important, the observance of Jewish rituals, or a true ethical life in which rituals may sometimes be overshadowed?

The Reform movement in Judaism more than a century ago sought to eschew ritual and concentrate solely on the ethical precepts. Practically every observance—the kindling of Sabbath candles at a prescribed hour, men's wearing of a head covering, abstaining from work on the Sabbath, kosher dietary laws—was set aside. Instead, the Reform movement noted with pride and reverence that the ethical teachings of the biblical prophets formed a powerful, eternal message for Judaism. Many rituals, however, have now been revived in Reform congregations. At a Reform temple men wear yarmulkes, candles are kindled to welcome the Sabbath or a holiday. No matter how idealistic or lofty-minded people might profess to be, they clearly need some kind of ritual, some physical displays that are linked to the past, to buoy up their own religious commitment.

Although most biblical prophets conceded that ritual observance can help people to lead a more religious life, there were some prophets—Amos and Jeremiah, for example—who suggested that such practices impede ethical living. In other words, by following rituals, people could avoid pressing social issues that properly demanded their immediate and full attention. In one famous passage, Amos quotes God as saying, "I abhor your sacrificial rituals." Jeremiah went so far as to claim that the animal sacrifices which were performed up until the destruction of the Holy Temple in Jerusalem, were really not to God's liking. Taken to its logical extreme, this would mean that one of the Five Books of Moses—Leviticus—is either superfluous or a false addition.

One of the unfortunate results of the earlier extremist position taken by the Reform movement against ritual practices, which even included the Bar Mitzvah and circumcision ceremonies has been the adamant refusal of traditional Orthodox segments of the Jewish community even to consider making any adjustments or amendments to Jewish religious practice.

The Conservative movement in American Judaism, numerically the largest of the Jewish community's religious groupings, has traditionally taken a stand somewhere between Reform and Orthodoxy. The very term Conservative was adopted decades ago to stress the movement's desire to conserve Jewish traditions, and at the same time to adapt Judaism to the new life evolving around the Jewish people, especially in the western world. The Conservatives always note that change—according to Halachah, Jewish religious law—has always been featured in Jewish life, and that indeed the entire Talmud and all the rabbinical commentaries and interpretations are simply reactions to a changing world.

Most thoughtful Jews, laymen and rabbis alike, would probably agree that although Judaism should place emphasis on the eternal prophetic teachings, most if not all of the traditional ritual should also be maintained for it helps immeasurably to give form and substance to the ethical lessons.

As one rabbi, Ephraim Rubinger, has said: "Jewish ritual, because of its antiquity and its aura of mystery, is able to reach into the deepest recesses of the human personality in a way that verbal intellectualization cannot. This gives ritual its healing power, and this power is particularly evident during moments of the life cycle which are traumatic and jarring— illness and death, marriage and children. By providing rituals that guide us during these difficult and confusing moments Jewish tradition allows the personality to maintain its emotional integrity."

* * *

The essence of religion is, in the words of Rabbi Mordecai Kaplan, "the human quest for salvation." The great rabbi and scholar of Babylon, Saadia Gaon, writing more than a thousand years ago, said: "The Bible is not the sole basis of our religion, for in addition to it we have two other bases—one is the fountain of reason, and the other is the source of tradition."

The story is told of a German Jewish conscript in the final years of the nineteenth century. His officer asks him, "What is your religion?" The young draftee hesitates, thinks, and then replies: "Sir, the Christians have a religion. We are Jews."

Judaism is far, far more than a religion. It is a whole way of life that encompasses a person's daily activities, twenty-four hours a day, seven days a week, and seeks to make that person as ethically good as possible. There are ritual practices, study sessions, regular worship, rules that are to be obeyed, words of deep spiritual significance which are to be uttered—in short, means by which life will be elevated to ever-higher plateaus.

Even a superficial perusal of the Bible will reveal a basic truth about Judaism—this is a faith that likes to tell it as it is. The biblical characters that are part and parcel of the western world's heritage are presented frankly, truthfully, with all their warts as well as their good features. The Bible includes Job and Lamentations and Ecclesiastes, which asks, "What profit has man for all his toil under the sun?" But the Bible also has all the other books, which affirm the worth of life, and stress its sanctity. "Saving a life supersedes the Sabbath," Jewish tradition declares. The historian Joseph Klausner said that the German philosopher Schopenhauer, greatly admired by the Nazis, hated Jews and Judaism because "he could not forgive Judaism for its affirmation of life."

* * *

Christianity is built around the figure of Jesus, while the central motif of Judaism is the law—the Torah, the Talmud, the oral tradition. A scholar declared that while Christianity is constructed around an ideal person, Judaism is a religion of ideals.

Judaism does not attribute divine status to Moses, nor any of the prophets, sages, rabbis, or great scholars. Only God is holy, only God may be worshiped.

Technology is applied science. Science alone, it must be clear, can do nothing for the world, for society; it must be applied, transformed into practical purposes.

The same is true of Judaism. The proclamation of lofty goals is not enough. These must be clothed in day-to-day practice. Hence, the emphasis in Judaism on *mitzvot*—religious commandments. The performance of these deeds will itself transform the doer into a loftier, better person.

This heavy stress on deeds in Judaism is a philosophy that has been followed through the centuries. Thus, a committed Jew knows that if he is a co-creator with God in this imperfect world, he must strive to improve society; he dare not look away and pretend that the evil is not there. A committed Jew knows deep in his heart that it is probably much easier to ignore Judaism's rules and regulations, to skip study classes, not to show up for services, not to contribute to a worthy cause, not to visit the sick or bereaved. But he also knows that if he does observe Judaism's laws and traditions, if he does perform all the mitzvot, if he does study and participate in congregational worship, he will become a better person, more at peace with himself, and with God.

* * *

Some non-Jews at times express astonishment at the strong attachment that Jews display, in the closing years of the twentieth century, to Israel. Anti-Semites of course accuse Jews of being more loyal to Israel than to America, a charge that is too ridiculous to even merit a reply. (It probably makes these anti-Semites enraged to know that it is now perfectly legal for an American citizen to be both a U.S. citizen and simultaneously a citizen of Israel).

To fully understand Jews and Judaism, it is essential to understand the Jewish people's fierce commitment to Israel. The late Abraham Joshua Heschel, a great theologian of the twentieth century, a charismatic rabbi who escaped the Nazis in Poland by a matter of weeks, and years later in America marched arm-in-arm with Martin Luther King, Jr., demanding full equality for blacks, once wrote his innermost thoughts on visiting Israel:

"We are tired of expulsions, of pogroms; we have had enough of extermination camps. We are tired of apologizing for our existence. If I should go to Poland or Germany, every stone, every tree would remind me of contempt, hatred, murder, of children killed, of mothers burned alive, of human beings asphyxiated.

"When I go to Israel every stone and every tree is a reminder of hard labor and glory, of prophets and psalmists, of loyalty and holiness. The Jews go to Israel not only for physical security for themselves and their children; they go to Israel for renewal, for the experience of resurrection.

"Is the State of Israel God's humble answer to Auschwitz? A sign of God's repentance for men's crime of Auschwitz?

"No act is as holy as the act of saving human life. The Holy Land, having offered a haven to more than two million Jews—many of whom would not have been alive had they remained in Poland, Russia, Germany and other countries—has attained a new sanctity."

GLOSSARY

Aravah	Willow branch used in Sukkot festival.
Ashkenazim	Jews from central and eastern Europe.
Ba'al Tshuva (Ba'alei Tshuva—pl.)	Newly-religious Jew. Literally, penitent.
Bar Mitzvah	Thirteen-year-old Jewish boy's religious coming of age ceremony.
Bat Mitzvah	Religious coming of age for girl, either at 12 or 13.
Cantor	Religious leader who conducts musical, vocal part of service. Often also teaches, leads chorus and can assist rabbi at rites of passage (wedding, funeral etc.)
Chalah	White, fluffy bread served at Sabbath and holiday table.
Chateemah Tovah	"May you receive a good sealing-in!"—a wish extended prior to Yom Kippur.
Conservative	One of three major wings of American Judaism, usually described as midway between Reform and Orthodoxy.
Diaspora	Wherever Jews live outside of Israel.
Dreidel	Spinning top played during Hanukkah.

141

Etrog	Citron, used during the Sukkot festival. Also pronounced as Esrog.
Grogger	Noisemaker, used mostly by children during Purim reading of the Esther scroll; noise is meant to drown out name of Haman, festival's villain.
Hadas	Myrtle, used during the Sukkot festival (with Lulav).
Hassid	Ultra-Orthodox Jew who wears distinctive clothing, and usually is devoted follower of Hassidic Rebbe or leader.
Havdalah	Saturday evening ceremony marking separation between Sabbath and regular work week.
Kaddish	Mourners prayer.
Kiddush	Blessing over wine recited on Sabbath and holidays.
Kosher	Pure, literally; in keeping with Jewish dietary laws.
K'teevah Tovah	"May you be inscribed for a good year"—pre-Rosh Hashanah wish.
Lulav	Palm frond, combined with willow and myrtle and used during Sukkot festival.
Ma'ariv	Evening service, recited daily; usually combined with afternoon (Mincha) service.
Maccabean	Referring to Maccabees, heroes of Hanukkah festival who cleansed and rededicated desecrated Holy Temple.
Mazel Tov	Congratulations! Good luck!
Menorah	Candelabrum; symbol of Judaism dating back to Temple days
Midrash	Non-legal, homiletic parts of biblical commentary.
Mincha	Daily afternoon service.

Mitzvah	(Pl.—Mitzvot) Religious commandments; also regarded as good deeds.
Ofruf	Groom's special honor in synagogue, before wedding
Oneg Shabbat	A Sabbath celebration, usually held in synagogue.
Orthodox	Strictly traditional form of worship and observance. Adverse to ritual changes.
Parsha	Weekly Torah reading in synagogue.
Passover	Oldest Jewish holiday, celebrating freedom. Most widely observed Jewish festival. Also known as Pesach.
Purim	Feast of Lots, commemorates Queen Esther's success in foiling plot to kill all Jews in ancient Persia.
Rabbi	Literally, a teacher. Spiritual leader of a congregation.
Reconstructionism	A small wing of Judaism close to Reform that seeks to eliminate supernatural aspects of Jewish faith.
Reform	Nearly two centuries old, Reform Judaism stresses ethics and is open to all kinds of innovations—including gay/lesbian rights.
Responsa	Religious answers given to people posing specific religious questions.
Rosh Hashanah	A two-day holiday marking the Jewish New Year.
Sabbath	Saturday, the Jewish day of rest; known in Hebrew as Shabbat.
Sabra	Native-born Israeli.
Seder	Festive Passover meal-cum-service.
Sedra	Weekly Torah reading in synagogue.
Sephardim	Jews from Spain and Portugal.
Shavuot	Pentecost festival, marking the Giving of the Torah at Sinai.

Shiva	Week-long mourning period.
Shmini Atzeret	Eighth day of Sukkot festival.
Simchat Torah	Festival marking launch of weekly Torah readings.
Sukkot	Fall festival, marked by eating meals in a sukkah—a simple hut symbolizing life's frailties.
Tallit	Prayer shawl. Also called a tallis.
Talmud	Combined commentaries of Bible, compiled over period of centuries.
Tefilin	Phylacteries, used in daily morning services.
Torah	The first third of the Jewish Bible. Also used to refer to entire Jewish religion.
Yahrzeit	Anniversary of loved one's death.
Yarmulke	Skullcap. Also known as Kipah.
Yeshiva	Religious academy
Yizkor	Memorial service.
Yom Kippur	Day of Atonement; holiest day in Jewish calendar.
Zionism	Movement seeking to reestablish Jewish homeland in Palestine.
Z'mirot	Songs sung between courses at Sabbath table.

144

A CHRONOLOGICAL
HISTORY OF THE JEWISH
RELIGION

(*Note:* B.C.E. means before the common era; C.E. refers to the common era, and is equivalent to the better-known form, A.D.)

Approximately 2,000 B.C.E.	Progenitors of the Jewish people migrate from Mesopotamia—today's southern Iraq—westward, to eastern shore of Mediterranean region.
Approximately 1,200 B.C.E.	Early period of patriarchs, development of tribal groups.
1,200 to 1,050 B.C.E.	Israelite slaves escape Egyptian bondage, follow Moses to Promised Land. Receive Torah at Sinai. Conquer and settle Canaan area.

1,050 to 970 B.C.E.	Jewish kingdom rises; long rule of King David. First Holy Temple built by David's son, Solomon.
About 1,000 to 586 B.C.E.	Rise of prophecy, development of early religious institutions and literature. Around 720 B.C.E., Assyrians attack, conquer Samaria region, exile ten northern tribes. In 587, Babylonians attack Judea, destroy temple in 586, exile Jews to Babylon.
About 540 B.C.E. to 70 C.E.	Jews return home, rebuild temple, prophecy takes on new vigor. Judaism now concentrates on Torah as law, and commentaries of sages. Meanwhile, Syrian-Greek power rises, demands cessation of Jewish worship. Led by Maccabees, Jews revolt, and cleanse and rededicate desecrated temple. Ascetic Jewish sect springs up, while Jewish community in Alexandria experiments with new forms of worship. In time of Philo, effort is made to merge Jewish and Greek cultures. Pharisees also rise, rejecting Hellenism, demanding pious and studious approach to Judaism. Romans

expand hegemony, conquer Judea, destroy second temple in 70. Rabbinic Judaism ascends, stressing scholarship and interpretation of Jewish texts.

90 to about 500 C.E.

Rabbi Johanan ben Zakai convenes Yavneh gathering to decide on canonizing Bible. Rabbi Judah the Prince edits the Mishna, the transcribed commentaries and rulings of the sages known as *Tannaim*. Major yeshivas are established to compile vast quantity of commentaries on Mishna (to be called the Talmud), resulting in production of both Babylonian and Jerusalem Talmuds. Non-binding, non-legal Midrashic commentaries—folkloristic, poetic, homiletic—also abound.

8th to 18th centuries C.E.

Legal concepts, liturgy of worship, and traditional text of Bible are set down. As result of Roman conquest and exile from homeland, Jews now scatter eastward, also to North Africa and to Spain. Jews come under influence of Christians and Moslems, and at same time experience

violent anti-Semitism.
Massacres take lives of Jews in
Rhineland, England, France,
Spain, Poland. Jews are exiled
from England, France, Spain,
Portugal. Talmud is publicly
burned in Paris and Italy.
Venice introduces ghetto.
Despite constant threat of
oppression, major Jewish
philosophers and scholars
flourish—in France, Rashi
(11th century), in Spain,
Maimonides (12th century).
Perhaps as reaction to dangers
and hardships, Jews turn to
mysticism as an added
dimension of Judaism.
Talmudic study in Eastern
Europe is intensified. Across
the Atlantic, first Jewish
arrivals settle in New
Amsterdam in 1654, marking
start of American Jewry—
largest Jewish community in
history.

18th century C.E. to present   French revolution,
development of *Haskalah*
(enlightenment), launching of
Zionist movement and initial
settlements in Palestine,
growth of Reform,
Conservative movements,
upsurge of Hassidism, violent
anti-Semitic pogroms in

Czarist Russia, onset of anti-Semitism in western countries in wake of economic depression, rise of Nazism and Holocaust, rebirth of Israel, and its emergence as second largest Jewish community in world and widespread increase in Jewish religious, cultural, and nationalist movements. On eve of 21st century, Judaism faces new challenges, many of them based on centuries-old issues of faith and identity.

BIBLIOGRAPHY

Leo Baeck. *Judaism and Christianity*. Philadelphia: Jewish Publication Society, 1964.

Bernard J. Bamberger. *The Story of Judaism*. New York: Union of American Hebrew Congregations, 1957.

Nathan A. Barack. *The Jewish Way to Life*. Middle Village, N.Y.: Jonathan David Publishers, 1975.

H. L. Ben-Sasson. *A History of the Jewish People*. Cambridge, MA.: Harvard University Press, 1976.

Philip Birnbaum. *A Book of Jewish Concepts*. New York: Hebrew Publishing Company, 1964.

Ben-Zion Bokser. *Judaism and Modern Man*. New York: Philosophical Library, 1957.

Louis Finkelstein. *The Jews: Their History, Culture and Religion* (vols. 1 and 2). New York: Harper and Brothers, 1949.

Saadia Gaon. *The Book of Beliefs and Opinions*. New Haven, CT: Yale University Press, 1948.

Harry Gersh. *The Sacred Books of the Jews*. New York: Stein & Day, 1968.

Nahum N. Glatzer. *A Jewish Reader*. New York: Schocken Books, 1946.

Will Herberg. *Judaism and Modern Man*. Cleveland: World Publishing Company, 1959.

Joseph H. Hertz. *Authorized Daily Prayer Book.* New York: Bloch Publishing Company, 1948.

Arthur Hertzberg. *Judaism.* New York: George Braziller, 1962.

Louis Jacobs. *The Book of Jewish Belief.* New York: Behrman House, 1964.

Paul Johnson. *A History of the Jews.* New York: Harper & Row, 1987.

Abraham J. Heschel. *A Passion for Truth.* New York: Doubleday, 1973.

Mordecai M. Kaplan. *Basic Values in the Jewish Religion.* New York: Reconstructionist Press, 1957.

Abraham J. Karp. *The Jewish Way of Life.* Englewood Cliffs, N.J.: Prentice-Hall, 1962.

Menachem M. Kellner. *Contemporary Jewish Ethics.* New York: Hebrew Publishing Company, 1978.

Francine Klagsbrun. *Voices of Wisdom.* New York: Pantheon Books, 1980.

Milton R. Konvitz. *Judaism and the American Idea.* New York: Schocken Books, 1980.

Moses Maimonides. *The Guide for the Perplexed* (translated into English). London: Routledge & Kegan Paul, 1881.

W. Gunther Plaut. *The Torah Commentary.* New York: Union of American Hebrew Congregations, 1981.

Dennis Prager and Joseph Telushkin. *The Nine Questions People Ask About Judaism.* New York: Simon & Schuster, 1975.

Dagobert D. Runes. *The Jew and the Cross.* New York: Philosophical Library, 1965.

Charles and Bertie G. Schwartz. *A Modern Interpretation of Judaism.* New York: Schocken Books, 1976.

Leo W. Schwarz. *A Golden Treasury of Jewish Literature.* Philadelphia: Jewish Publication Society, 1937.

Abba Hillel Silver. *Therefore Choose Life* (vol. 1). Cleveland: World Publishing Company, 1967.

Milton Steinberg. *Basic Judaism.* New York: Harcourt, Brace & World, 1947.

Herbert Weiner. *The Wild Goats of Ein Gedi*. New York: Atheneum, 1954.

Herman Wouk. *This Is My God*. New York: Doubleday, 1959.

Michael Wyschograd. *The Body of Faith*. San Francisco: Harper & Row, 1989.

INDEX